INVESTING
IN THE
RIGHT
PROPERTY
NOW!

MARGARET LOMAS

First published in 2011 by Major Street Publishing Pty Ltd
Reprinted 2013 and 2016
© Margaret Lomas 2011
The moral rights of the author have been asserted

National Library of Australia Cataloguing-in-Publication data:

Author: Lomas, Margaret.
Title: Investing in the right property now!/Margaret Lomas.
ISBN: 9780987084910 (pbk.)
Notes: Includes index.
Subjects: Real estate investment. Finance, Personal.
Dewey Number: 332.6324

Internal design by Production Works
Cover design by Principle Design
Printed in Australia by SOS Print & Media Group

10 9 8 7 6 5 4 3

Dedication

'True love is when you put someone on a pedestal,
and they fall – but you are there to catch them.'
UNKNOWN

To my husband Reuben. I have fallen so often that sometimes
there are only small pieces to pick up – but still you pick
them up and pile them back on that pedestal. There are
no words to explain what you mean to me, and to do
justice to the myriad ways you make my life worth living.
Thank you. I love you.

ACKNOWLEDGEMENTS

Whenever people tell me about how they feel I have helped them, I have to remind them that no one could possibly achieve anything in this world without great support from others, and I am no exception.

For many years now, I have had a great team of Destiny® branch managers who devote much of their lives to assisting people whose imaginations I ignite and who become motivated to buy property after reading my books. They go out of their way to ensure that people get things right and I owe a huge amount of gratitude to them.

In our head office everyone does what they can to accommodate me as I fly in and fly out, always busy. I can rely on everyone to help me when I need it, and we have a great team of truly dedicated professionals.

My long suffering family still makes me feel like less of a domestic failure whenever I feel sorry for myself. My children, now virtually all adults, have an amazing sense of tradition, and are so very close to each other. It's such a magnificent pleasure to watch your children grow into mature and confident adults, and I have received the greatest blessing of all in this family I have been given. And so to Mark, Kristy, Belinda, Michael and Rebecca, I love you all so much.

I never separate my children out as they are all equally special to me. However, Kristy is also my PA at work, and her capacity to achieve all I need her to, and her support of me, is what keeps me on the road. She steps in as mother more often than I care to admit, too.

There are a few other people who inspire me greatly, too.

Noel Whittaker – you like to say you made me what I am today! In truth I am inspired by your example, and so privileged to feel like a member of your own amazing family.

Neil Jenman – thank you for fighting the good fight and for never giving up. When I feel weak I remember how hard you fight and I fight on another day too. Thank you for your constant words of encouragement.

Terry Ryder – for being one of the very few property experts whose opinions I value – thank you for all of your help.

Ian and Trish Spruce, my *Property Success* editors, who remain committed to the project through thick and thin and who are a joy to work with – thank you!

And to the board of the Property Investment Professionals of Australia (PIPA) – thank you for being there as we fight the bad guys and plug away until the government finally gives the industry what it needs – regulation. I promise we will get it in the end!

WHAT PEOPLE SAY ABOUT MARGARET'S BOOKS

"I have to tell you that I have been searching for this type of information for quite a while. It was pure pleasure reading your books, knowing that I had finally found someone who is able to look at property investing from a holistic viewpoint and who has a thorough understanding of the subject. Your ability to communicate this information simply and clearly is commendable and I found I was able to easily follow and understand what you were saying.

"My goal has been to have 20 investment properties before retirement and I now know how to achieve this goal, thanks to you. I would just like to say thank you! Thank you so much for putting sanity into the otherwise insane practice of property investing."

KIM AYERS

"I have just finished reading your book How to Create an Income for Life *for the second time, and I cannot commend you highly enough for putting together such an easy-to-read and even easier-to-understand guide to positive cash flow property. Thank you for taking the time to share your wealth of knowledge on the investing topic with the general public. Without people like you who want to help others learn and succeed, it would be so difficult for people like myself to even know where to start. After reading your book, I feel that much of the fear and uncertainty created by a lack of knowledge has been buried forever, and I am even more excited about property investment as an option for securing our future than I ever thought possible."*

SALLY HUDSON

"It all started with your book back in 2001 ... I have to pinch myself from time to time! I thought it was time that I thanked you for your books, particularly the first one, which got me started.

"My wife Rosalie thanks you also. She was very apprehensive about retirement, just couldn't see how we would get by.

"She is once again the woman I married. We are both freed from the financial burdens that plague the general populace. When I whistle while I work, people look at me strangely. Is being contented a lost sense?

"Thank you and keep up the good work. I promote your books to everyone I come in contact with."

CHRIS AND ROSALIE VINE

"Thank you so very much for sharing your wisdom, knowledge and experience with everyone. Through your efforts and the domino effect, you are going to be responsible for improving the future lives of many, many people, all over the world, mine included.

"Thanks so much, Margaret, for your work and support in the world of investing."

GARY AND KATHY KLARENDECK

"What a happy task it is to say that I was delighted to read your book A Pocket Guide to Positive Cash Flow. *I found it informative and easy to read and understand. Well done!"*

PR

"Thanks again for being such an inspiration."

SC

"I have found your book easy to understand and look forward to reading your others ... thank you for sharing your knowledge with people like myself. I don't know if you could ever realise how much hope you have given me.

"I hope I am right in saying that you have written your books because you really care. One day may I be able to give some of this back to somebody else."

SS

"Out of all the people I've come into contact with in the property industry, you are the only one I would really trust. Good on you, Margaret!"

PM

"Just finished reading How to Create an Income for Life – *a great book, Margaret. It really brings property investing into perspective and I learnt a lot from it. Unlike other books that leave you feeling as though you can make a million in a few months, this book sticks to reality and, sometimes, reality sucks! But it is real and having read several books on the subject, this is one of the best I've read to date. Well done, Margaret."*

DF

"I have just finished reading your book How to Create an Income for Life *and loved it. I have read quite a few investment books and found yours to be the most inspiring. I really came out of every chapter feeling uplifted (unlike a lot of the others I have read)."*

SG

Also by Margaret Lomas:

How to Make Your Money Last as Long as You Do,
Wrightbooks 2001

How to Create an Income for Life, Wiley 2002

How to Invest in Managed Funds, Wiley 2002

How to Maximise Your Property Portfolio, Wiley 2003

Pocket Guide to Investing in Positive Cash Flow Property,
Wiley 2004

The Truth about Investing in Positive Cash Flow Property,
Wiley 2006

20 Must Ask Questions for Every Property Investor,
Wiley 2008

CONTENTS

PREFACE

It's been three long years since I wrote my last book. During that time I have been asked more often than I can count, 'when are you writing another book?'

I've always been quite sure that I would never write another. Just how much can one say? Having written six property books, I'd had a good go at unloading my philosophies upon the investing public, at times with an element of controversy and always with a great sense of passion. From a creativity perspective, I have been getting my fill creating and producing my television show, *Property Success with Margaret Lomas*, and I've certainly been kept busy with its filming for the past three years. I truly lacked the motivation to write again, and having little more to add to what I had previously said didn't help matters.

But, around a year ago, I started to sense a big change on the horizon in terms of how we buy property. Most likely motivated by the post-Global Financial Crisis (GFC) confusion about exactly where, how and indeed *if* we should continue to invest in property, I began to more closely examine the property landscape. I started to question much of what was being said, and has been said, about property investing. As I fielded more and more questions from investors who were finding that the strategies of old were simply not working out for them, I knew that I had to know more about the dynamics of buying property so that I could better advise both my readers and my viewers.

And so I set about comprehensively considering the

economy, property and the future for Australia, and, slowly but surely, I began to become excited again. I was finding that there was so much more to explore, so much more to learn, and that doing so was going to uncover ideas and information which no other property expert had really ever seemed to consider or had disseminated.

And so, here I sit today, head bursting with information which I can't wait to share. Anyone who passes my office gets an earful as I enthusiastically grab them and babble about how we should all be learning new ways to buy property, essentially challenging all the theories and smashing those myths which have been fed to us for far too long. It's the 21st century and it's high time we began to act and think like we live in *this* century, rather than the last!

Let me start this book with one very important thing that I have learned resoundingly over the past 12 months:

It's not so much time in the market as it is market timing!

If you feel that statement is exactly opposite to that which you have heard spruiked by property advisers and experts the country over, then you are right – it certainly is. However, all I have learned since the GFC has proven to me, in many ways, that market timing is the most important consideration for all property investors. As you read on, you will see how market timing involves so much more than simply buying in a low market and selling in a high one, and being lucky in the timing of when you buy property.

Be warned – this book isn't going to go easy on you. It will challenge your thinking and require you to have that most unpalatable of lessons – the economics lesson. I aim to show you how, once you can understand the dynamics of how macro and micro economies operate, you will be able to use this knowledge as a solid base from which to choose the next hotspot, before it becomes one!

I'm not going to go into the basics of property investing: how to research, finance and structure your next purchase. I've already done that in many of my other books and the information in those books is just as relevant as it ever was. If you are new to investing, it won't matter if you read this book first, but you will need to read some of the others as well to round out your education (please see the further reading section at the back of the book).

Instead I am going to present to you an entirely new set of criteria which will help you to become a better investor than you have ever been before. It will bring you into the 21st century and ensure that you will always buy the right property, NOW!

Margaret Lomas
June 2011

1

WHAT ARE WE REALLY
DEALING WITH?

Wherever you look, and whatever you choose to read today, someone will be commenting on what people see as our one, singular property market. Newspapers emblazon the headline 'Property market to crash!', while the nightly news features another story about the dismal auction results and the underlying health, or otherwise, of the 'Australian property market'.

I have a particular dislike of this propensity to group all property into seemingly one awkward monster which has behaviour that is both predictable and consistent across the entire country. I gather that the reason this occurs is because, in reality, despite the fact that the shares of many different companies really should perform differently from each other, and in fact do so while ever there is a stable sharemarket, a stock market crash sends all stocks plummeting regardless of any underlying strength an individual company may have. The need to apply similar logic and performance behaviour to the property market surely springs from this leading example.

We also cannot ignore the impact of sensationalist reporting upon our perceptions of the property market. On a slow news day, we're likely to see reports of shaky or crashing property markets, with no clarification to advise that, in fact, the information was sourced from data gathered from just one area or city. When the Melbourne newspapers scream 'Worst property performance in 15 years!', we naturally think it means *all* property, when in reality it could be referring to the Melbourne market, or even a small pocket of the Melbourne market (most likely the 5 kilometres around the journalist's own home!).

Such a view of how property behaves can actually make a market all on its own. If we hear often enough that property is crashing, it may well become a self-fulfilling prophecy. As investors, if our fears are fuelled by evidence presented by those who we deem to hold particular authority, like economists and reporters, we may then exercise caution toward that asset class until we hear brighter news. It's a little like rewarding the negative behaviour of a child, and that child repeating the behaviour because this reward leads them to believe that the behaviour is acceptable. We stay away from property because of what we have read, and, if enough people subsequently abstain from buying, what we have read becomes true – property crashes!

> If we hear often enough that property is crashing, it may well become a self-fulfilling prophecy.

The very first thing which you must learn, early on, is that Australia is made up of literally hundreds of markets, and these smaller, individual markets will behave according to their own cycle. In addition, that cycle may be *counter cyclical* to adjacent markets, and it may also be *counter cyclical* to the overall economy. Many times, during the years in which I have invested, I have seen the markets I have purchased in bucking the overall region's trend and growing in the face of stagnation everywhere else.

To invest well, and to invest often and consistently, you must know that at any one time, you *can* find a market which is about to enter a significant growth phase, and you *can* use information and your own skills to determine where such an area is. Then, with what you know about your personal circumstances, you can match a property to your own personal needs as perfectly as you can match two black socks!

Later in this book, I'll show you just how that happens, and what you need to do to improve your chances of getting it right. Before then, we have to lay the groundwork and help you to have a solid foundation in economics, and a reasonable expectation about what can be achieved through property investing.

What you should NOT believe

In my writing and on my television shows I provide information about the latest schemes and scams being promoted to property investors, to issue a warning to those of you who may be looking to either fast-track your own investing, or rely on the assistance of someone else to help you to put in place a suitable strategy. Some of the latest schemes are covered in Chapter 14.

Here though, I'd like to start with some of the more common investing strategies which are still being promoted. This should help you to see that investing in property has fundamentally changed, and a strategy which was being promoted in 1990 isn't going to provide you with the best possible investment property in 2011 and beyond.

I'm constantly surprised that experts who hold a relative amount of stature within the investing community are still repeating that which has been said for as long as I can recall.

A strategy which was being promoted in 1990 isn't going to provide you with the best possible investment property in 2011.

It's as if today, if you'd like to be considered an expert, just sing the same tune as someone from the old days and then write a book (making sure your photo is on the cover in living colour!). You'll have an instant following and another generation of investors who are unhappy with their property investing, and who continue to perpetuate the rumour that property makes a substandard investment vehicle.

To enable me to introduce some information which will greatly improve your investing success, here are some of the ideas which are being suggested. Later, throughout this book, you'll see just how off the mark they really are, and how following them will limit your success as a property investor.

Blue chip properties, in city CBDs, grow best

This is an old one, and one which I certainly cannot believe is still being promoted. Those who insist that only Central Business District (CBD) properties qualify as blue chip property, and only blue chip property grows well, clearly do little real research and are overlooking the significant evidence which proves that it is not the location, per se, which impacts on how well a property grows. While location may play a small role in property choice (which occurs last in the purchase process), initially there are an abundance of factors which actually play a vital role in whether an area, and so an individual property, will grow well, or not.

I've purchased property in many areas, but only two within a CBD of a capital city. In our entire portfolio, these two have had the worst performance. Amongst the rest, some have been exceptional and some have been 'good', but these two CBD properties have had, overall, the lowest rates of growth and provided the lowest yields. They have grown in value since I purchased them, and I am not suggesting that they have been bad purchases. However, the properties that I have chosen elsewhere have consistently outperformed these two, because they have a greater number of growth drivers. (We discuss growth drivers further in Chapter 6.)

The regions have good cash flow but lower growth

While the regions definitely do often show a better rental yield, most probably due to the lower buy-in prices and the relatively higher rent returns, it doesn't follow that they also perform less well in terms of their capacity to grow in value as a result of these higher yields.

...most CBD and coastal properties showed the most lacklustre growth of all.

In his '2009 Iconomics Report', Terry Ryder, a property journalist with a wealth of knowledge and significant property experience, prepared a study covering the prior 15 years, examining property growth. This study proved empirically that many regional areas had experienced exceptional growth for the period, and that most CBD and coastal properties showed the most lacklustre growth of all.

So, while it's true that 'location, location, location' may be the key to good growth, it's not true that there is any link between that premise and the location being the seaside or the city. The characteristics that make property grow well have nothing to do with whether it is in the city or the country. Both the city and the country can grow well, and both can grow poorly. It is a host of other factors which determine the growth, and we will explore these later in this book.

You have to buy median priced property, or greater, to do well

When an area grows well, it is usually the result of what I call 'intrinsic' growth drivers. Intrinsic growth drivers are those qualities of an area which exist *within* an area – factors which are sustainable and ongoing, such as population growth, infrastructure planning and economic vibrancy (more about intrinsic growth drivers later).

When an area exhibits an abundance of such drivers, all property in that area will grow well, regardless of whether it is low-priced or median-priced. Having said that, the higher the price, the less well the property will grow. This is because, as prices increase, less people are able to afford to buy property with higher price tags, and more people fall into those lower price brackets. Usually, this places more pressure on lower priced properties, and I have found that, as long as the area as a whole is growing, lower priced properties will achieve the best growth rates of all property in that area.

Therefore, once you have found the right area, and qualified it according to all of the things you will learn in this book, it's more likely that you will achieve a greater result from properties purchased in the lower end of the market than you will from those which are median-priced or higher. There are some small exceptions to this rule, and I will be sure to cover them for you.

The cash flow/growth choice

I receive a lot of email from investors with questions about where, and what, they should buy at any one time. Usually they will say something to the effect of "I'd like to buy something that is going to have good growth in the next five years", or "I would like to purchase a property with a high yield".

When you think about this, it's really a moot point. I can't imagine that anyone would write and say "I'd like to buy property that doesn't grow well, one that has a low rental yield!"

I consider that the whole point of buying property as an investment is to see an increase to the value of the asset, and the greatest possible income from that asset during the time that the investor owns it. My guess is that, when I receive such email, the writer believes that they cannot have both cash flow and growth at the same time. The 'experts' have created this misconception by continuing to validate the theory that a property can only have one of these characteristics, either cash flow or growth.

While some property has good growth with low yields, and others have good yields with low growth, the best property is that which has both!

This is simply not true. Throughout this book I aim to show you that while some property has good growth with low yields, and others have good yields with low growth, the best property is that which has both! Further, buying property which has both is not only highly possible, but such property always exists somewhere, regardless of the present state of the economy.

As an investor, your goal must be to ensure that each

property you purchase provides the best possible growth, for the best possible rental yield, during the period that you own it. You want your purchase to have its best performance – its greatest period of growth and most attractive rental yield – just after you buy it. In Chapter 4 I take an in-depth look at both cash flow and growth, and explain what you really need from your property investing.

Getting the cake and eating it too

If you have ever watched the live show which I host on the Sky News Business Channel, *Your Money Your Call*, you have probably listened to the large number of viewers who call in to ask about an area in which they are considering investing. Often, it may be a well established area with solid values, and at times the area may also have acceptable rental yields. Many wonder why I recommend against such a purchase when it seems like a good place to buy.

The reason is simple. For most investors, investment property will be purchased one property at a time. Very few people have the financial capacity to go out and add a large number of properties to their portfolio at once. This means that each and every property purchased must represent the best available opportunity at that time, and in the five to ten year period immediately after it has been purchased.

Many areas that I may recommend against may indeed be stable areas in which to invest. The investor most likely won't lose, and will probably experience reasonable growth while they own the property, as long as certain basic criteria are also met. But remember this: Buying any one property means that you don't buy something else which may be a far better proposition! A purchase in one area will always carry an 'opportunity cost', and where property is concerned the opportunity cost is missing out on another area which more than likely would have delivered better growth and higher overall rental yields.

Still, value growth and yield growth are often cyclical in nature, and except in rare cases, hardly ever occur at the same time in one area. In the prior section I discussed the fact that investors do not need to choose whether they want property which has cash flow or growth because you can get property which will experience both at some time in the period you own it. The trick becomes finding a property which has not yet had a significant increase in *either*, so that both can occur while you own it. Later, I will explore exactly how this works, how you can choose the right property for you based on where in the yield/growth cycle it exists when you buy it, and which one of the two you need to occur first.

Market timing

You'll often hear property experts and those trying to sell investment property use the phrase, "It's not market timing, it's time in market".

My theory is that this is said to help you deal with any short-term negative performance that the property they sell experiences! When someone is giving you property investment advice based around a single area in which they may have available stock, the likelihood that *that* exact area is the best available investment *at that moment in time*, and is the closest possible match to your own individual investing needs, is pretty unlikely. I am not saying that those who sell investment property only sell poorly performing property (although some most certainly do). I am suggesting that properties sold by property investment advisers are unlikely to exactly match what you need, nor will they likely be in the best hotspot available.

In any event, if you keep any property long enough (with a very few exceptions), the sheer time that you remain in the market will most likely smooth out short-term negative growth and cash flow losses, and the property will ultimately be worth more than you paid. Whether its future value is high enough to have made the overall performance strong or not is another thing, and often once you consider the holding costs, the overall returns can be dismal indeed.

In order to build the best possible property portfolio that you can, one which outperforms the average and contains properties which consistently deliver high returns, giving the greatest possible growth during the time you hold it, market timing is the key. You want to find an area on the verge of its boom, and have that boom occur during your period of ownership, and you want this to occur with every property you buy.

Sound impossible? I don't believe so. While a very small element of luck may be involved when you do buy property, you can ensure that each property you buy is the best available at that time, and you can reduce the part that luck plays in your investing. However, you must be diligent, understand what drives growth and be prepared to do a lot of very hard work to narrow down your choices. You can time the market and you can significantly reduce your chances of buying a property which fails to perform well while you hold it.

Knowing the area

I have mentioned this frequently in my other writing and market commentary over the years because its importance is relevant. When you've known me long enough, you'll realise that there are constant facts which I will repeat over and over again. This is because these particular facts are important, and they will not change over time.

Don't fall into the trap of believing that you should only buy in the area where you live because it's an area that you know well. When people insist to me that they must at least start by buying in their own area due to its familiarity, I play a little game with them and I ask a range of questions about their area. In virtually every case, I discover that the person has very little knowledge about the most common growth drivers in their area, and what they actually 'know' relates to lifestyle features.

What you know about your area includes information relevant to you as an owner occupier. While this also becomes important for a renter – your potential future income-producer – this information is by no means the catalyst by which an area will achieve that 'better than average' growth. The information most crucial when you are looking to invest in an area is data which local residents are unlikely to know about their own area.

It's also unlikely that you will be lucky enough to be living in the area which, at the very moment you are about to invest, is among the top hotspots of the country. While I have seen it happen, more often an investor, particularly one using home equity to leverage into an investment portfolio, will live in an area that is coming *out* of its major boom phase. They have most probably been able to grow equity in their own home because their area grew really well, but by the time they decide to use this equity, the area has settled into its stabilised growth phase and it will begin growing *less* well than other potential areas.

Always remember that you don't have to live in an area to know it well. By the time I buy in any area, I can guarantee that I 'know' it better than the locals do. What I know about that area, though, relates to economics, and what the locals know is more likely to relate to lifestyle. Lifestyle features rarely create boom towns, whereas economic vibrancy is the cornerstone of a future hotspot.

Always learning, always changing

It's prudent to make note here that few areas remain a hotspot for years on end. That is not to say that an area becomes the wrong choice – remember earlier I suggested that many areas I recommend against are solid areas and buying in them will not be a poor choice – it may just not be the best choice you can make, *at that time*. Remember that each purchase carries an opportunity cost, and that cost is that you may miss an area about to experience its greatest period of both values and rental yield growth.

The other important factor that all investors must know is that the window of opportunity to buy in a hotspot is always quite small. When I present my list of hotspots at my seminars around the country every year, I do so with a warning that, if anyone is going to procrastinate before they act on the information, it's crucial that they confirm whether or not the information is still valid and the window is still open when they do eventually act. All hotspots settle down to become one of those stable areas, and once this happens there will be another, better area elsewhere.

Economic vibrancy is the cornerstone of a future hotspot.

At those same seminars someone always raises their hand to ask my opinion about investing in an area which is not on my list, and which does not show significant growth drivers. My response is always the same – if it's *not* on the list, I think it's probably *not* a potential hotspot.

Summing it all up

It's for all of these reasons that investors can't afford to subscribe to a single property investing theory and expect that it will last for their entire investing lifetime. I wrote some things 10 years ago which were just right, back then! Over the years my message has changed and evolved, not because I found out I was wrong, but because the investing landscape has evolved. Property investing requires a constant process of education and updating of information, and investors who aren't prepared to undertake it will find that they do not succeed as well as they possibly can.

By all means, listen to every theory, but as you do consider it as it applies to how we live today. Take into account a range of factors, the most important of which is that we live in a constantly growing country where the needs of the population vary, and where technology presents a vast change to how we live, work and play. This wide brown land of ours grows smaller as we grow closer together through an array of technological advances which are made on an almost daily basis. As such the way we buy property is bound to change, and keep changing. It will only be those investors who are prepared to let go of these archaic theories and appreciate that the new world needs a fresh new approach who will achieve the greatest degree of success.

~ Australia is made up of thousands of property markets which all behave according to their individual micro economies.

~ 'Blue chip' refers to property with a strong prognosis for growth and cash flow – it does not refer to CBD property exclusively.

~ Properties outside of CBD areas can have equally good growth and have, in many cases, had better growth.

~ Median priced property in any area does not perform better than property in the lower price bracket.

~ You do not have to forego cash flow to get growth, or growth to get cash flow.

~ While 'time in market' is important, an investor can improve their results by also timing the market well.

~ A property investor can choose a property which will have cash flow growth *and* value growth though the two are unlikely to occur simultaneously.

~ To 'know' an area from an investment perspective is not to 'live' there. Adequate research can help an investor to 'know' any area.

~ The window of opportunity to buy in a hotspot is small.

THE PROPERTY
LANDSCAPE

I t still seems like only yesterday that we were all in a panic,
worried about the Global Financial Crisis (GFC) and
holding back from investing just in case it was the end of
the secure financial world as we knew it. For a time the
world was in economic freefall and some of the greatest
economies of our time were brought to their knees in a
crippling meltdown, the likes of which we had never before
experienced.

Here in Australia, it took us a little while to come to
grips with the whole thing, and for a long time, in our
enviable Aussie style, we all refused to accept that we would
in any way be affected by the events which were bringing
the global financial world to its day of reckoning. Amid
reports of toppling economies, we here in Australia
continued to spend, enjoying the last remnants of the good
times in an almost steadfast refusal to allow any of the news
to actually bring us down.

The Reserve Bank, desperate in its attempts to administer
monetary policy ahead of any trouble, kept on hitting us

with interest rate rise after interest rate rise, but it took a long time to actually have any impact.

While we may have avoided a major catastrophe, I still believe that it is a huge mistake to think that nothing has changed. It was the steadfast refusal of many Americans, most notably those in the financial services industry, to believe that property moves in anything other than one direction (and that is up) which ultimately undid an entire economy. It's an economy which is still in the grips of disaster, and it's anyone's guess as to where it will finish. We might be on the brink of seeing one of the world's strongest economies become the weakest, and the standard of living of most Americans is likely to be impacted for many decades to come.

We should be learning some valuable lessons from this experience. It's time to take stock, and a reflection upon where property has been is useful for us to prepare for where it's likely to head. In examining what has happened to property and why, we can actually draw valuable conclusions about the significant role that the economy plays in the health of the property market. And while I certainly have grown tired of listening to the dire predictions of economists as they attempt to overlay pure economic theory to the property market, I do see that a solid understanding of the economy at both a macro and micro level may be the most powerful weapon that a property investor can have at their disposal.

A solid understanding of the economy at both a macro and micro level may just be the most powerful weapon that a property investor can have.

What has happened so far?

As we emerged from the immediate threat of the GFC, much speculation still surrounded our property markets. From my perspective, the major problem with the reporting of the situation was that it was coming largely from unqualified observers, usually based in capital cities, who were commenting on the area immediately around where they were situated as if it was a true indication of the entire market as a whole. Consequently, as buyers were breathing a sigh of relief at having avoided a total economic meltdown in this country, and were once again beginning to enter the market, property at the higher end of many capital cities began to slowly move again. And so spurted forth a frenzied period of reporting that led many investors into falsely believing that the market had been saved and high priced, inner city property was back on the hotlist.

Meanwhile, and without much notice, outer suburban and regional markets quietly percolated away. Having stabilised after the removal of the first home buyer stimulus and multiple interest rate rises, pundits were mistakenly reading this short period of inactivity as a downturn in these markets. Yet, while the frenzied buying into swank city apartments and coastal properties began to once again throw that market into turmoil, these quiet achievers, which I like to think of as bread-and-butter properties, began to do their stuff, and the results were fabulous.

Looking at the situation as a whole, a clear pattern was emerging. While those more expensive properties delivered a higher growth, in short bursts, during periods of strong investor sentiment, cheaper areas with strong intrinsic growth drivers subsequently surged ahead. They finished up completely smashing their higher priced counterparts, that had settled down to actually record much lower growth, and in many cases negative growth, overall.

While there is much to learn from this, and I will explore just what this means to you as an investor as this book progresses, the first conclusion that we must draw is that in good times and in bad, bread-and-butter properties, appealing to the lower end of the market, will always perform – as long as the growth drivers exist.

> In good times and in bad, bread-and-butter properties, which appeal to the lower end of the market, will always perform.

In my own portfolio of well over 30 properties I enjoyed significant benefit from the GFC. I've always stood quite alone on my side of the property investing fence – the side where I buy in outer suburbs and regional areas, purchasing lower priced property which deliver yields of at least 6%. The criticism of my philosophies has been pretty loud over the years, with predictions that my penchant for such property would mean that growth would be fleeting for me.

Just before the GFC hit I had 14 properties valued so that I could free up some equity. I was overall quite happy with what I was told – two properties had not moved a lot in two years but twelve had definitely grown. Since all had excellent yields I was happy with this result. Interestingly enough, the two which had not moved were the two most expensive in my portfolio – the ones I had indulged in knowing that I wasn't quite being true to myself.

Fourteen months later, and post GFC, I had the same properties valued yet again. Across the 14 properties I had seen a total value increase of $400,000, and this was taking into account the fact that those nasty two high-end properties had actually lost $40,000.

The good news doesn't end there – throughout the GFC the twin effect of interest rate cuts and my ability to increase rents on the entire portfolio, since my properties were in such a high demand sector of the market, improved my personal cash flows by $150,000 per year.

If that's a GFC, bring it on! In all seriousness, we don't want another GFC at all, but indeed if we are to face more uncertain economic times, as I firmly believe we shall, there are some lessons we must learn.

'Cheap' property

Many years ago I was painted by some as being the property expert who purchased cheap property in far flung regional towns which may have had good rent returns but rarely had much chance of any real growth. I've since been able to prove that particular rumour to be completely untrue. In fact, except for my first lemon investment purchase, I have yet to buy a property which hasn't doubled in value in at most five years, with many doing so in three.

> Buying property well isn't actually about buying 'cheap' property…

However, it's still thought that my preference is to buy cheap properties just because they are cheap, and this is far from the truth.

Buying property well isn't actually about buying 'cheap' property at all. A lot of 'cheap' property performs very badly indeed, simply because it exists in areas with little going for them. If you are using the purchase price as a guide to what you should buy, then you are using the wrong strategy. The price of a property has little correlation to its ultimate growth, whether that means that you have bought really cheaply or, conversely, in an expensive market.

I had a friend email me once to ask me for my latest tips about where to buy property. He had made the decision to commence his property portfolio and, since he knew me, figured that, rather than waste time on education, he should just pick my brains about where to buy. After cautioning him against plunging into any investing strategy without a suitable amount of research and education, I provided a location in NSW which I had recently visited for a town spotlight for my show, *Property Success*. It was an area where I believed some great growth drivers existed. He emailed back with the comment: "Shouldn't I be looking for property with a higher buy price, maybe in the city?" He simply could not accept that there wasn't a relationship between purchase price and growth potential. He figured that the more he spent, the greater his return would be. I was sure to let him know in no uncertain terms that there's absolutely no empirical evidence whatsoever to suggest that growth is in any way linked to buy-in prices. Some really expensive properties grow badly, as do some really cheap ones. Some really cheap properties grow really well, as do some really expensive ones.

Instead, choosing a property which is going to satisfy your need for both values and rental yield growth involves buying property which will remain in demand by renters to keep the yield strong, and also in demand by buyers to keep the value strong. In my considerable experience, this type of property is situated in *any* area where intrinsic growth drivers exist. (Examples of growth drivers include infrastructure planning, a growing population, increasing median household income and economic vibrancy and we discuss these further in Chapter 6.) Being 10 kilometres from a CBD, near the beach, city or country, cheap or expensive is all actually moot – if the drivers don't exist, the property won't grow consistently and sustainably. If drivers do exist it will, despite much of what is happening economically to the country, or the opinions of market commentators.

Think back to my experiences with my own property during the GFC. Property markets everywhere seemed to be cooling, and many people stayed out of the market altogether, waiting to see what would transpire.

My properties were situated in areas rich in growth drivers. I had chosen them based on the level of infrastructure development in the years to come, being sure I always chose those areas where the money for those plans was already in the bank, rather than sitting on a wish list somewhere. I picked towns or suburbs deep in the heart of diversified industry where unemployment was low – areas where industry wasn't seasonal or reliant on a growing economy, but was strong in manufacturing and providing the staples which a population needs come hail or shine. My purchases had always been in areas where families lived, worked and played and where the micro economy was skipping along in a healthy fashion.

When the GFC hit, it affected those who held higher priced property – some needing to sell to ease financial stress. In these areas it became difficult to find a buyer and so they began to stagnate. Those who were buying began to look for more affordable property in areas where I held my property! And renters, who poured into the market at a great rate of knots, stormed my bread-and-butter properties causing demand to push rental yields higher.

The fact that most of these properties were highly affordable when I bought them wasn't the reason I bought them. I bought them because they paid for themselves with a strong weekly cash flow and displayed an equally strong capacity to keep the demand rolling through good times and bad. And, not only did this work, but it worked contrary to what economists and experts were predicting at the time, and contrary to how the macro economy was performing.

The media

I've already alluded to the fact that enthusiastic press reporting can often shape the direction of the market. I think that a good lesson to learn from the past few years is to largely ignore the press reports of what is happening where property is concerned. I have friends in the media, and I do know several journalists who are indeed worth every cent they are paid and more. These journalists will report what is happening with clear and qualifying statements about the market on which they are reporting, and how they came upon their information.

Mostly, though, it's about the story, and creating a front page headline which sells papers. You'll hear how first home buyers all over Australia have given up the dream of ever owning a property. Then if you read the fine print you'll learn that this statement was based on a survey of 56 first home buyers and 30% of respondents had given up all hope of being able to ever save a deposit. This is hardly a majority! In other reports you might hear that property is in a bubble which is about to burst, only to discover that the story is based on a couple of $5 million

> Investors often become spooked by headlines and stay out of the market.

mansions which can't be resold for anything more than $3.5 million. And, sadly, this kind of sensationalist reporting can almost become a self-fulfilling prophecy. Just as Chinese whispers spread like wildfire with an ever-changing story, investors often become spooked by such headlines and stay out of the market. Ultimately fiction sometimes becomes fact, and this is not good for anyone.

Another issue with much of what we read in the press is that

Property doesn't really behave in any kind of trend.

it is typically historical reporting. When a report refers to a market which is falling, it will be based on figures collated from the prior six or 12 months, and rarely upon forecasts about the future. Even where forecasts are used, how are these forecasts made? – by using past figures to estimate a trend when property doesn't really behave in any kind of trend. Rather, property responds to drivers in the market-place which can happen sporadically, or consistently. The best thing about such reports is that they can provide a reliable indicator of where *not* to buy. If an area is reported as having had some stunning growth, it's most likely to now have prices which are beyond affordable, and the opportunity to buy is probably gone.

Finally, much of what we read in the press is subjective, and refers to one, most probably very small, market. We have thousands of markets around this country, and each one responds to the drivers which exist in their own geographical area. Wise investors examine the area microscopically and realise that while one area may be flattening, another may very well be starting its boom.

Economies

Later in this book I'll be discussing economies and showing how the greater economy provides the backdrop against which property will perform, or not. It's important to know that a micro economy can, and often does, perform at odds with a macro economy. While a country may be reporting a falling gross domestic product and a slowdown in economic growth, a single town or area may be in a growth cycle and experiencing a boom. Unemployment may be low and population growth may be at an all-time high, with business and industry booming.

We can read much from local economic data, and finding it, then using it when you are doing your research, is a skill which will set the astute investor apart from the average one. Most local councils publish an economic brief every year. This contains forecasts as well as details about economic development and council strategy for fostering growth. Once you know how to read, interpret and apply such data, you will be investing wisely, as a result of facts that you can know, rather than investing emotionally and according to how you might feel about an area.

> The greater economy provides the backdrop against which property will perform...

Property investment leader, or follower?

While I most definitely subscribe to the practice of ensuring that you have a good team of people to help you on your investment journey, it's just not enough to simply follow others in where and how they invest. You can't become a successful investor if all you ever do is attend seminars, buy what is on offer or listen to the secrets being spruiked as if they were gospel truth. If this is you, then you are only ever going to be getting the leftovers, or buying in areas where the person who makes the most profit is the one who sold the property to you.

When Trish and Peter came to my company, Destiny®, for assistance, they already owned six properties and seemed to be doing pretty well. They had purchased all of them from one adviser who had links with a developer. Therefore, all of the properties were in one area and all were very similar types of property.

> You can't become a successful investor if all you are ever going to do is attend seminars, buy what is on offer or listen to the secrets being spruiked.

In truth Trish and Peter were not really sure if they were good investments or not, and when we asked them about why they had purchased them, they couldn't really answer the question. It was fantastic that they had seriously started to invest, but there were a number of issues:

~ All the properties existed in the one area, which meant if that one area slowed down, all of their properties would also slow and further leveraging would be difficult.
~ Most investors, after purchasing six properties, would be becoming more knowledgeable and self-sufficient, but as Trish and Peter had relied totally upon this one adviser it meant that they were not developing as investors. Investors who develop skills along the way are more likely to be those who also recognise hotspots before the crowd does.
~ In Peter and Trish's case, they had also met significantly higher buy-in costs due to commissions

along the way. This placed them further behind in terms of equity acquisition.

While you must have expert guidance and input, and gaining some good education and mentor support is a crucial part of the plan, you also have to know how to approach the task on your own, and find the areas and properties which are most likely to do well, despite what is happening in the overall economy. Your adviser or mentor can't be with you every minute of the day. Sooner or later it's important to be able to find the areas and make property choices on your own. You won't do this if you have to constantly ask someone else where to buy or what to buy. Only when you learn how to do your own research, validate what you find and then interpret the results in terms of what makes good buying, will you begin to experience the kind of success which sets a successful investor apart.

> Gaining some good education and mentor support is a crucial part of the plan.

That's not to say that you must become an island. I know from experience that success is enhanced when you have the support of the right people, and when you spend some of your time, at least, networking with like-minded people, attending quality events and adding to your knowledge on a regular basis. My company Destiny® has thousands of clients, many with similar financial circumstances but all with vastly different success rates with their property investing. They all have access to the same level of knowledge and support, but we have found that those who attend everything we offer, and seek out support on a regular basis, are those who have the most success.

Make the decision today to become as educated about how to buy property as you possibly can, and then commit to a plan which allows you to in some way work upon your property investing strategy every day. By being in what I call the 'property headspace' as often as you can, you'll become a property investment leader with an exceptional portfolio and a secure financial future.

And so...

As you read this book, try to keep an open mind and cast off the lessons you have learned about how to buy property up until now. Forget the mantra 'location, location' or at least begin to understand that this is not a physical reference, it is a reference to whether an area is perfect for investing in now, or not.

From here you must know that there is not a single strategy, method or theory which works all of the time for property. Instead, what *does* work is understanding why and how a property can grow, and then setting out to find exactly that kind of property, every time.

> Become as educated about how to buy property as you possibly can be.

And then, when you add the next property, do it all over again and find the next hotspot. Oh, and keep this book handy when you do – it will become your best resource!

KEY POINTS

~ The GFC *has* impacted on how we buy property.

~ The price of a property has no correlation to how well it grows.

~ Media reporting can give a false reading on how property in specific areas is behaving.

~ Much reporting is based on historical figures, and such figures do not reflect what may happen in the future.

~ Property does not behave in trends.

~ Understanding and determining economic data is a valuable skill for all investors.

~ Continuous education and exposure to property information will keep you ahead of the others.

AN
ECONOMICS
LESSON

3

When I went to school I hated economics. In fact if I remember correctly, economics was the lesson that I always managed to wiggle out of, using the excuse of a dentist's appointment, ill health, or possibly I just 'wagged' that lesson. It was always after lunch, when I, like most, was at my energetic worst, and the teacher seemed to drone on endlessly about facts which I could see no use for in the future.

Now I wish I'd paid more attention, as I may have been able to build a stronger property portfolio much earlier than I have. Little did I realise that these lessons would form the basis of how to recognise a hotspot and buy in the best areas, all of the time.

I've become so excited about the application of this subject to property investing that I now need to share these same lessons with you. Be warned, this information isn't overly compelling, but it is an important part of the groundwork that you need to lay, so you'll just have to bear with me.

Before I do so, remember to temper this information with everything else you know or are learning about how to buy property well. No single factor makes up the decision to buy any property, and it is more the 'concert' of factors which will help you uncover a good area in which to buy. Where one feature of an area or region is looking promising, other factors may exist to counteract that feature and turn what appears to be a potentially good area into a poorly performing one. You need to be utilising all of the information and looking at a wide array of factors prior to making a decision to purchase anywhere. This economics lesson will provide the broad backdrop against which you can proceed to obtain more specific information. It is your crucial starting point every time you buy.

No single factor makes up the decision to buy any property.

Economic factors and their influence

Gross Domestic Product (GDP)

If we take a small village of people whose only occupation and income source is to make baskets for the bigger city nearby, we are able to estimate the level of productivity, and whether or not this is growing, by considering the total retail value of the baskets they sell. If, in one year, the village realises $50,000 from basket sales, and the following year it realises $52,000, then their local economy, or productivity, has grown over that year by 4%. There could be several reasons why it has grown – it may be a result of the increased price of baskets, and the growth has come from inflation, or perhaps more people have started making the baskets, and so more were sold.

In a similar way, the growth of the economy of a country can be measured by looking at its Gross Domestic Product (GDP). GDP is a term which describes the market value of all final goods and services produced within a country in a given period. It is often considered an indicator of a country's standard of living.

GDP includes the following components:

~ **Consumption** is a measure of all of the final household consumption expenditure in the economy. Personal expenditure is further categorised into durable goods, non-durable goods, and services. Consumption doesn't include the purchase of new housing.

~ **Investment** includes business investment in new business and business assets, but it does not include the exchange of existing assets. The private purchase of new housing is also included in this category. Investing in a financial product is *not* included in this category as this is classed as 'saving'. This is because if it is counted in investment it may be double-counted – if you buy a share in a company and that company buys plant and equipment, this investment would be counted twice.

Growth of the economy of a country can be measured by looking at its Gross Domestic Product (GDP).

~ **Government spending** is the sum of government expenditure on final goods and services. It includes salaries of public servants, purchase of weapons for the military, and any investment expenditure by a government. It does not include any social security payments.

~ **Exports** represent gross exports (total value of all exports), since these things become part of another country's consumption but are produced here.

~ **Imports** represent gross imports (total value of all imports). This is deducted from the figure, since if it's included it will then be considering foreign supply as domestic product and skew the figures.

There are three ways that the GDP of a country is calculated, but they pretty much all deliver the same result:

1. *The product approach* determines the total actual market value of all goods and services produced within the country.

2. *The expenditure approach* determines how much is actually *spent* on the goods and services of the country. It assumes though, that everything that is produced will be bought.

3. *The income approach* determines how much income is received by the people who produce the goods and services – that is the prices paid for them and received as income.

It's a little bit of economical madness to have three ways to calculate this because when you look at them you realise that they are actually measuring exactly the same thing – the result will be the same however you look at it!

The diagram opposite shows how money flows, with the solid arrows indicating the components of the GDP.

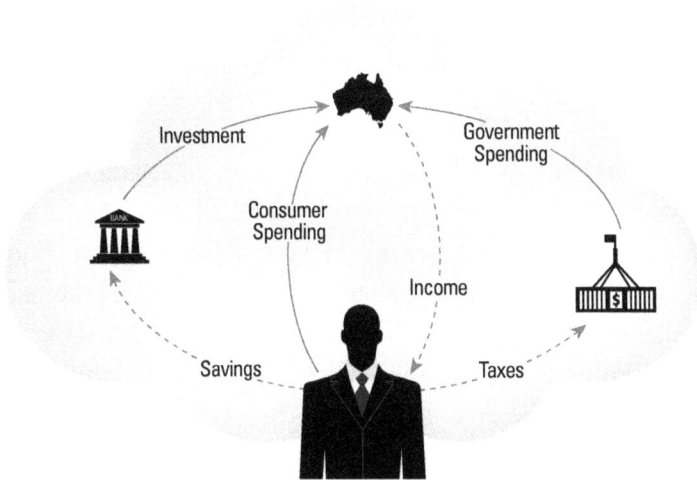

Once it's been calculated, GDP is usually a figure which is quoted in the billions of dollars. This is then compared against the last time it was measured, and the difference is expressed as a percentage. This figure represents the amount by which the economy is either growing or, in the case of a negative figure, shrinking.

You don't really have to know what the country's GDP is, or how it's calculated, or what it is even measuring. The reason why it is important for you as a property investor to be aware of GDP is that it expresses economic growth, and economic growth can be forecast according to GDP figures. Where the country is experiencing strong economic growth, it will have a positive change to its GDP figure. If we are producing goods and services and the country is spending money on them, and the figure from one measurement period is higher than that from the prior one, then economically speaking we are turning over, and progressing. Where the GDP figure is in decline and lessens from the prior measurement period, then we are most likely spending less, and not producing, and so the economy is shrinking.

How does GDP relate to property?

In earlier chapters I have talked about the fact that we do not have one, singular property market. I also mentioned that some areas can and do behave counter-cyclically to others, and to an entire macro economy. Therefore, considering whether our nation's economy is growing or shrinking isn't of any great value when you are looking to buy in say, Bathurst, because Bathurst may have a very different economic picture.

What is important to know, though, is that GDP can be considered at a local level, both through Gross State Product (GSP) and Gross Regional Product (GRP) figures. As with GDP, which is measuring the growth, or otherwise, of an entire country, the growth of a state and a region can be reflected in GSP and GRP figures and trends.

Now here is where it gets tricky – it's important to access GRP figures as well as the GSP and GDP, and then consider them in terms of the trends, and how they compare to each other. (I tell you where you can find these figures towards the end of this chapter.)

Firstly, it is desirable for the area you are researching to have a GRP which is growing. Where recent figures show that the regional economy is shrinking, look for the reasons why and determine if it is the result of underlying economic uncertainty in that area. For example, where a major industry that formerly employed a large portion of the local population closes, the next reporting period may show a decline in the GRP. Further investigation would be required to assess the reasons behind the closure – it may have been a problem with that industry, an issue with the local area, such as an inability to obtain the right kind of workforce, or a lack of market for the products. Such investigation will assist in determining whether or not this will be a lasting situation, or just a passing phase.

Secondly, you will want the GRP growth of an area to match, or exceed, the GDP growth of the country (in terms of percentage). Where it is less than the country's GDP, then you may be looking in an area which is lagging behind the rest of the country in economic growth. The chances are good that such an area will also lag behind the country in growth in property values too.

A strong, growing GRP may be a precursor to other economic factors which ultimately drive property growth.

Lastly, you want the GRP to be trending upward – that is, growing a little more each year. As a backdrop to the overall health of the area, a strong, growing GRP may be a precursor to other economic factors which ultimately drive property growth – more jobs, a growing population and increasing median household income. Examined alone, GRP may seem a little insignificant, but examined in concert with many other factors, which we will outline throughout this book, a sound GRP should place a big tick on the 'pros' side of your property investing checklist.

Employment

It seems obvious that we should all consider buying property in areas with low unemployment rates. Where there is a considerable lack of employment, an area can quickly become unstable and people can eventually move away. Areas with high unemployment typically suffer from other issues too – higher crime rates and lower GRP rates.

A high unemployment rate doesn't always spell trouble, and employment data must be examined for both its rate in relation to the national average, and for its trend.

An area with unemployment rates lower than the national average is an area which also has economic vibrancy. That being said, it is important that you thoroughly examine what this employment represents so that the 'concert' creates beautiful music over the long term, rather than just a fabulous show for an hour or so!

Strong employment in an area where there is only one major industry may offer a false sense of security – while everyone has a job at the present moment, many would not have a job if that one industry suddenly failed. On the other hand, strong employment over a diverse range of industry types is a sure sign that the economy is vibrant and able to withstand short-term issues, such as closure or stagnation of single industries.

> An area with unemployment rates lower than the national average is an area which also has economic vibrancy.

Further, a strong employment figure which is under-pinned by jobs growth, showing a downward trend in the unemployment rate, is even better. Remember, you are seeking an area which is more than just 'solid' – you want it to be about to become a hotspot. Where employment is on the increase and jobs are growing, other factors often follow – population grows, there is pressure on rents and, eventually, on house prices.

In addition to that, the more jobs there are, the more productive an area becomes. Productivity often translates into spending, and as long as the services exist to meet the demand from the demographics of an area, that spending is likely to occur *within* that area. If a population is able to cycle its wealth back into its own micro economy, by earning and spending locally, this is a further boon to GRP growth.

Jobs growth

Aside from underpinning continued employment growth, jobs growth has another, often ignored, impact on the economy as a whole.

When jobs are becoming less available, employees tend to remain in their jobs longer. When there isn't much work about, this is a sign of a slowdown in the economy. Employers begin to rationalise costs, cut jobs and expect each worker to become more productive. Employees wanting to keep their jobs may work longer hours and ask for fewer pay rises. The cycle gradually grinds to a halt and the situation impacts back on the greater economy.

Conversely, when job availability is growing, employees have more choice. They begin to exercise this choice by applying for, and moving to, better or more diverse positions and employers find staff turning over. Since the cost to employ and train new people is often great, the preference is to retain the employees they already have. The best way to do this is through wage increases.

And, as job vacancies grow, so does the collective wealth of the country. People earn more, spend more and become more able to manage and plan for interest rate rises. Businesses produce and provide more to meet this improved demand, and they begin to pay more to their employees, who spend it back on those same goods and services. Property becomes more affordable, not because its value drops, but because wages are on the increase and buyers can afford to support

> As job vacancies grow, so does the collective wealth of the country.

larger loans and pay higher rates of interest, removing a large impediment to house price growth.

As with all economic factors, jobs growth can occur locally, even in the face of a national decrease in the availability of work and an increase in unemployment. Typically we will see this occurring in those areas where other significant growth drivers exist – for example, strong infrastructure development, a diversification of industry and the provision of improved services to local residents. As a barometer to the overall economic health of an area on a micro level, jobs growth is an excellent indicator of improving economic vibrancy.

Industrial and commercial property markets

While many property investors will never consider buying a commercial or industrial property, the role such property plays in improving the economic potential of an area cannot be overlooked.

Where commerce is strong, companies large and small often spend their money on commercial real estate, preferring to own rather than rent. This creates a demand for commercial and industrial space which impacts on prices.

Where the value of industrial and commercial property is growing generally, signs exist to indicate that the underlying economy is in a prosperous phase. Commercial and industrial properties are generally valued according to the yields they can bring. Basically, if a commercial property can bring high yields, its value will grow. Where the yields fall, so does the value of the property.

While this is different to residential markets, where the value is not usually impacted by the volatility of yields, what is common between the two is the fact that it will be demand from tenants which drives the yield growth. If commercial property is in demand, this will usually be an indicator that business in general is thriving – more people getting into business will create more demand for commercial and industrial space.

If commercial property is in demand, this will usually be an indicator that business in general is thriving.

On a more local level, where the demand for commercial and industrial space is pushing up yields, the indications are that business is growing, either from within, or as a result of large companies moving into the area. Business growth equals jobs growth, and jobs growth equals economic vibrancy.

Of course it goes without saying that economic vibrancy then translates into an area becoming more populous, more affluent and, especially if there is already a shortage in housing, property prices will grow.

Housing starts

This term refers to the number of new private dwellings where construction has commenced in a given period. It is most often measured quarterly.

As a measure of economic health, an increase in housing starts over three to four measurement periods is usually a good sign that the economy is coming out of the doldrums and is once again in a growth phase.

However, for property investors, by the time such a statistic is measured and reported, that window of opportunity to buy into a potential hotspot may be lost.

From your perspective, you will want to see reports of low housing starts in the face of positive economic indicators elsewhere. Where the low figures relate to high unemployment, low population growth and slow growth for business, then this could be an indicator of a declining or stagnant area. But where an area shows economic vibrancy BUT low housing starts, it's definitely a big tick in the 'pros' column of your hotspotting checklist.

Growth in overseas visitors

How often have you bemoaned the influx of tourists to an area where you may want to enjoy a quiet holiday? Well, next time you find yourself wishing that they would go home to their own country, stop and think again!

When an Australian resident spends money on goods and services, the money they use to do this has come at a 'cost to earn'. The original dollar first of all funded the cost of production of the goods or provision of the services. It then incurred taxes, and bills were paid from it. Finally, what is left of the dollar is spent and injected back into the economy.

When an overseas visitor spends money in Australia during a visit, the whole dollar is injected into the economy. The entire dollar is profit, as another country paid for the earning of that dollar. This is sad for them, as they paid for it and saw no return. It's great for us, as we get all of it for virtually no cost to us!

Considering this factor on a more micro level, a community which attracts more than the average amount of overseas visitors is one which will benefit more greatly from the tourist dollar.

Remember though, that this must be tempered against other factors which may reduce or even eliminate this benefit. Areas relying solely on the tourist dollar may experience seasonal swings in economic vibrancy, and many other factors which can make buying in holiday areas a bad idea. As with all growth drivers, this one must be considered alongside the other features of the area.

Council financial health and leadership

I've been travelling around the country for around three years now, examining areas for my TV show and presenting them in a segment which identifies those areas which are hotspots, and those which are 'notspots'.

In doing so I believe that I have uncovered another characteristic, which, while it may not be purely economic, certainly contributes to the likelihood that an area will utilise its potential and grow to become a serious hotspot.

Some of the areas which I visit definitely have some of the signs that they are heating up. They have affordable housing, people are moving to the area, and the opportunity to design and implement infrastructure plans is freely available, waiting to be taken advantage of.

Yet, when I speak to the mayor, or the staff, it seems no-one's driving the train. Lethargy exists and the desire to maintain the area at its present, sometimes parochial and small town status, pervades the council at every level.

Let me share an example.

I recently visited two areas, located relatively close together. Both have strong signs of potential growth and plenty of opportunity to maximise this growth with defined infrastructure plans. Prior to my visit I had assessed both as being potential hotspots – one immediately and one in the coming five years or so.

The mayor of the first area explained to me that they had identified that a significant proportion of their population was under 25 years of age and, as these people were their future, they needed to encourage them to stay to raise their own families. As such, council identified their needs as more important than those of the aging proportion of the community, and was focusing all energies on future developments which would suit this demographic. Initiatives included more medium-density housing, employment projects and the encouragement of small business ventures. Development application processes were also being streamlined to speed up new residential and commercial development and provide what was needed as quickly as possible. I left the area wishing that I owned more than one property there!

The mayor of the second area spoke of the importance of not embracing change too quickly so as to preserve the charm of the area. He was unaware of the significant opportunities afforded by the coming broadband roll out, and his council had no plans around utilising that opportunity. As a resident himself approaching retirement, he wanted to ensure that all of those features the aging population enjoyed remained intact. When asked if plans existed to improve the development application process in response to the needs of the community, he replied, "It's not about what they want, it's about what council wants and they must understand that we have a set process!" I left, and immediately reassessed my summary of that area and pushed out any potential growth by another five years!

Please don't misunderstand. There is nothing wrong with an area retaining its country charm and keeping the big smoke at bay for as long as it can. However, if this is what the plan is, then there can't be any complaining when the funding for that latest transport infrastructure project is not forthcoming, or when the local economy stagnates and eventually shrinks to being almost non-existent.

For an area to thrive, grow and prosper, its council must

be 'open for business'. The councillors must approach the task of management as if they are running a business, and they must doggedly set about bringing attention, funding and interest to their area.

This requires a whole host of tasks, and such a council must start at a grass roots level. They must consider their planning processes, how to foster and encourage business growth, how to facilitate residential development and implement master planning. They must think long term and plan for and encourage population growth. And, they must look at where they are at today, where they want to be in five and ten years' time, and then identify the gaps, or the barriers which stand in their way.

When I come across such a council, and also find that all of the necessary intrinsic growth drivers are in place, I get excited. It instils a confidence in me that the facts I have uncovered about that area are most likely to be exploited and given every chance to flourish, so that it can become the hotspot it has the potential to be.

Local government is at the absolute core of the economic engine of a community.

Local government is at the absolute core of the economic engine of a community. It has the power to fire up that engine and be in one of the top spots at the finish line, or to crash and burn and be an 'also ran'.

Where do I find this information?

Of course, this is where the hard work comes in. The kind of information which I have listed in this chapter comes from many sources, and your job will be to do the hard yards and try to harness it without working so hard that you wear out before you even buy a property!

Many councils have some kind of economic brief. You can either download this from their web page, or they can post a hard copy to you. In addition, many councils also now utilise census data and display demographic information on their websites. Take care that this data is not too old, as census data is only collected every five years.

Studies are often done by associations such as the Housing Industry Association so it's useful to check in on their website from time to time. Many of these studies are done on a national or state basis, though, and you will need to try to apply the information to the local areas that you are researching.

A plain old Google® search can usually uncover most of what you need. Always check the dates and scope of any studies you are viewing and ensure that reported data has not simply been extrapolated from an early study, as it is unlikely to be accurate if it has been.

And that's the canvas, ready to go

Of course, you are not yet ready to pounce and buy that property in the area where you have found sound economic vibrancy. At this stage, all you have done is decided whether your canvas is suitable to paint a picture upon. While it's rare for a great picture to be created upon substandard materials, many a fine canvas has had a tragic mess painted upon it, so much so that the original material is lost forever.

In researching this economic landscape you have simply uncovered those areas, usually entire regions, where potential exists. Now it's time to get much deeper, to allow you to decide once and for all if what you are reading economically has any chance of translating into property investing success. Read on to discover the paints, the brushes and the concepts, which will bring it all together.

~ No single factor makes up the decision to buy property – it's the 'concert' of factors which is important.

~ Gross Domestic Product is important for assessing the economic health of a country.

~ Gross Regional Product helps you to determine if an area is bucking the nation's trends.

~ Unemployment levels can provide reliable information about future economic vibrancy.

~ Jobs growth usually equals economic growth.

~ Industrial and commercial property markets can measure the health of business in an area.

~ Housing starts point to population growth.

~ International visitor spend can boost a micro economy.

~ Strong leadership at council level can be a crucial driving force behind ultimate economic growth.

MATCHING PROPERTY TO YOUR OWN NEEDS

If you have read any of my books, listened to any of my podcasts or read any of the articles I've written, you have probably heard the cash flow and growth debate so many times that, like me, you've become somewhat tired of it. With the abundance of up-to-date and economic information which is available today, I'm still amazed that people who claim to be property experts refuse to learn anything new, so that they may start teaching better and more prudent ways to buy property.

If you're new to the argument, it's a pretty simple one. Some properties have a really good rental yield, and some have really high growth. The argument centres on the premise that one property cannot have both and that in buying a property with one of those criteria, you sacrifice the other. It also suggests that property in regional areas will have higher yields (at the cost of growth) and that properties in the CBD of major cities will have higher growth, at the cost of yield.

This blanket, one-fits-all theory completely ignores so many things about modern property investing. It also ignores the significant changes to how we live and what we all are prepared to accept in terms of services which exist around us. Not everyone wants to live in the city these days, and technology has meant that few of us even need to *work* in the city any more. With large companies relocating to cheaper industrial land and the internet allowing us to do business virtually anywhere, our presumptions about what makes a sound property investment simply must change.

How it was

In the early days of property buying, people purchased property in the cities, where the employment, and the services, existed. Infrastructure occurred mainly in these areas, as did transport development, and people worked in the cities too. Entire communities were city-centric and many of us saw the CBD as the hub around which the outer suburbs essentially revolved.

Those who lived in the country did so for either lifestyle reasons, or because they were farmers. Many regional families today are descendants of farmers, even while they no longer work the land themselves. Because of this agricultural history, employment in such areas was normally restricted to farming or agricultural support industries, or in some areas, single industries such as mining.

These days, as the population of the country chokes the cities, it's become a crucial part of our landscape for people to begin to move outward to areas which are not necessarily city-centric. As such, we've seen the governing bodies of many regional and rural areas respond to the needs of these new generation inhabitants by providing services, infrastructure and transport which equal any capital city. Furthermore, cheaper base real estate prices in these outer areas have also made them a far more attractive proposition. This has resulted in the features of capital cities being seen in regional and rural areas, as well as in the far outer suburbs of those cities, and the property in those areas is responding with similar growth characteristics.

Those experts who are still spouting the 'CBD is best' theory are just plain wrong, and are clearly people who lack the economic knowledge to be able to understand the radical change in property value behaviour which the millennium has brought. As I've said, much evidence now exists to show that, for many years, CBD and coastal properties have in fact shown the most lacklustre growth of all property, which supports the fact that things are definitely changing.

> Those experts who are still spouting the 'CBD is best' theory are just plain wrong.

It's still important to understand the way property grows and what affects its yields. Doing so provides some useful hints about what to buy, in terms of its capacity for growth in value and rent return. The choice isn't about whether you buy city or regional property, it is about whether the time is right for you to buy property which is in its yield growth phase or its values growth phase. The other really important thing which all investors need to know is that the best kind of property you can buy will have *both* cash flow and values growth, at some time during the period you own it. Cash flow is the thing which will keep you in the market – a property with a good cash flow will less likely drain you of your personal cash reserves and make it easier to hold throughout all the economic ups and downs – while you need a property to grow in value to eventually make money from the investment.

Before I talk about how to choose what is right for you at any given moment, let's recap the two features, cash flow and growth.

Capital growth

Capital growth refers to the increasing value of a property over a period of time.

In the past it was always considered that property in the city would grow faster than that in the country or the regions. As I said before, this was because most employment was available within the major cities which boasted the best resources and infrastructure. Hence, more people lived in cities and demanded property there.

Since capital growth is directly linked to supply and demand, it is certainly feasible to expect that wherever there is a suitable demand for property, growth will be stronger than in an area where the demand is less. In areas where housing supply doesn't keep up with demand, we usually see values growing better than average. In areas where the supply fails to keep pace with the demand for a consistently long period of time, we see values grow steadily over those long periods.

While all of that is indeed true, what is not true is that those features which contribute to strong property price growth are only seen in capital cities. As explained, the changing face of how we live is applying certain demand pressure in many parts of the country, not just in the cities.

Where growth is concerned though, you don't want to buy in those areas which are subject to short-term bursts of growth, which we see happen in capital cities, usually due to investor sentiment. While it certainly seems like an excellent idea to buy property in areas with a high expectation of *short-term* growth, the problem for investors is that prices rise far more quickly than rent returns. While it may be typical for a property situated in a booming area to rise by 20 to 30%, it is likely that rental return will only keep pace with inflation, and increase by around 3% per annum. Eventually, rent return may catch up with values, restoring the balance, but this can take many, many years.

This is why timing becomes paramount when choosing an area with the best prognosis for growth in both its rental yield and its value, wherever that may be, and why it is still the key. If you buy the property after the values have started to increase but before the rent returns move, you will be likely to be supporting a sizable negative cash flow. While you wait for the rent returns to grow, you must make up the difference between income and expenses in the event that the property is geared (i.e. you have borrowed to buy it). In addition, you may not see more growth for some time, as many of these short bursts of good growth are often followed by lengthy periods of stability. This is because the growth is fuelled by sentiment or market pressure, without the underlying factors which result in consistent growth.

The other problems with buying property only for its growth, without considering all other aspects of the investment, are:

~ The investor's lifestyle may be impacted as funds previously available for personal spending are used to support the property, in the hope that the yields will grow.

~ The ability to buy multiple properties becomes limited to the surplus cash flow an investor has from their employment (which will decrease with each purchase).

~ It is a gamble – what will happen to the investor if they commit their personal funds but the anticipated growth does not occur?

Remember, even if after reading this book you eventually decide that you need to buy property entering its cash flow growth stage, property price growth is going to be important too. Cash flow will give you a weekly income, but this is limited to the amount of rent you have left after you pay all expenses and lodge all of your depreciation claims. Price growth, especially if it's been greatest in the period you own the property, can provide a range of options once you do retire – a lump sum, cash for living or those holidays, money for other investing or equity on which you can be earning rent return.

Cash flow

When you buy a property which is rented, you will receive cash in-flows in two ways. One will be the amount of the actual rent you receive, and the other will be the amount of the tax you have paid elsewhere that comes back to you after making allowable tax claims. When you add these two together, you get a gross cash in-flow amount.

Tax claims can be made for both the actual loss (that is the difference between income and expenses) and for the on-paper loss, which occurs as a result of depreciation on the fixtures, fittings and the building itself. When you claim the actual loss, you have essentially paid the money for that loss, and you can now claim it back. You can, however, only claim back a portion, in the same percentage that you have paid tax on other income. On-paper losses, on the other hand, while providing only a percentage of that loss back to you in a tax break, mean that you receive the tax back without having to pay any of it out.

From the cash in-flows, you must deduct all of the costs of holding that property, including the interest on any debt that you obtained to buy it. The balance is the cash flow. In some cases this cash flow might be positive, in some even, and in others, negative.

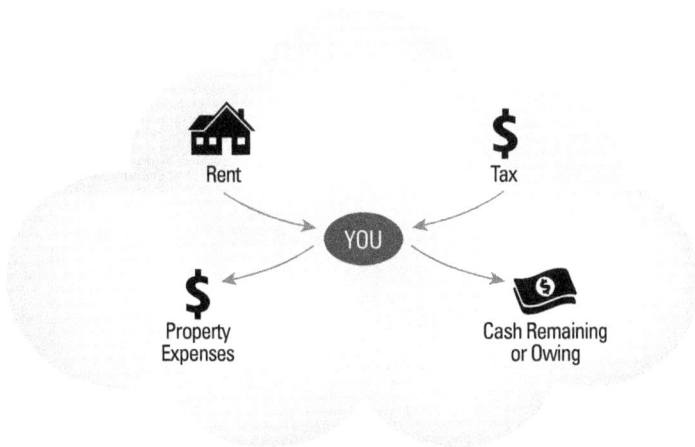

Depreciation

Some of you who are reading this book may not be familiar with the term 'depreciation'. Where it applies to an allow-able tax claim for an investment property, this is definitely one of those concepts with which you must become familiar. Understanding what it is, the types of property in which it will occur and how to use it to increase your cash flow, is really important.

It's a fairly in-depth topic, one which I have explored in detail in several of my other books. For now, here is the concept, in a nutshell.

Depreciation refers to the loss in value due to general wear and tear and the effects of time on the building, fixtures, fittings and furniture on an eligible, income-producing property. The property does not have to be new to make these claims, but the age of the property will affect both whether such claims are available to you, and what claims can be made. The website of the Australian Tax Office (www.ato.gov.au) includes a "Guide to Depreciation" which can be downloaded. This guide covers the dates during which a building must have been constructed to qualify for depreciation claims, and details of what may be claimed and at what rate.

Essentially, there are three components to depreciation:

1. **Capital works depreciation,** which is a deduction for the loss in value on the actual building
2. **Depreciation on plant and equipment,** which covers the fixtures and fittings not included as part of the structure; and
3. **Renovations and improvements,** or those items which were added to the original structure.

When you make a claim for a depreciation expense, you are claiming a 'loss in value'. You do not have to pay anything to receive this deduction, as essentially you paid for the items when you bought the property, completed the renovation or purchased depreciable items for the property. Since you receive a tax deduction, and so a tax refund, for this loss in value, it's a little like getting some of your tax back, without losing it to an actual payment of an expense. This is why a property which is eligible for this type of tax deduction is more likely to show a positive cash flow, or less of a negative one, than one which isn't.

You don't have to worry about working this out, since a quantity surveyor can prepare a schedule for you in which an estimate is made of the original value of all items and structures in the property you have purchased. Further, the complex calculations on any extra items you buy, plus how this will affect your tax deductions, will be done for you if you use www.destinylive.com.au, which is a complete online property portfolio management tool.

There is a great deal more to know about depreciation, and in the 'Further Reading' section you will see a list of those books which can help you.

Too many terms

Now, here is where it can become a little complex.

There is a lot of confusion about cash flows, much of which comes down to terminology. Often when people call me on TV to ask a question, or send in an email, they ask if they should use a *negative gearing* or a *positive gearing* strategy. To further complicate things, accountants talk of positive cash flow and negative cash flow. Let me see if I can assist by providing some simple explanations:

1. Negative gearing and positive gearing are not 'strategies'. They are, more simply, tax terms which describe a cash position outcome.

2. The strategy is 'property investing'. If you borrow to invest, the tax term is 'negative gearing', or 'positive gearing'.

3. Gearing means 'to borrow', and if you borrow to buy a property and the income is less than total expenses, this is known as 'negative gearing'. The tax office gives you back a little bit of this loss, to the extent of your marginal rate of tax (i.e. if you pay tax at 30%, you'll get back 30% of the loss).

4. If the expenses attached to purchasing and managing your property are less than the income it generates, this is known as 'positive gearing', and you'll pay tax on the difference to the extent of your marginal rate of tax (i.e. if you pay tax at 30%, you'll pay 30% tax on your gain).

5. To sweeten the deal, you may claim on-paper deductions such as depreciation. These on-paper losses also result in a tax refund to the extent of your marginal rate of tax (e.g. $1,000 of on-paper losses results in a $300 tax refund if you are on the 30% rate).

6. *Sometimes* the amount of tax that you get back, if it includes on-paper deductions, will be enough to make up the difference between what goes out (expenses) and what comes in (income). This is known as 'positive cash flow'. If this happens when your property is negatively geared, then you have a *negatively geared property with a positive cash flow*. Of course, a positively geared property has a positive cash flow at the outset, but your tax refund will make it more so.

To summarise:

~ Negative gearing = expenses greater than income
~ Positive gearing = income greater than expenses

~ Positive cash flow = when you are left with money after you make all of your claims. This can happen if you negatively gear (where you get a tax break big enough to make up the difference) or where you positively gear (where you are left with money after you have paid the tax).

To be honest, all that you really need to know is whether or not the area has the potential to allow you to buy a property which will more likely have a positive cash flow, or a negative one. Most of my books have complete details about how to work this out, and if you own any of my books you can download a free tool to calculate this for you at destiny.com.au.

How do you choose?

The old assumptions were that if you found a property that had a high positive cash flow, which also indicated a high yield in relation to purchase price, it would be in an area like a regional town, with potentially low growth.

But, as I said previously, this is no longer the case. Property with good yields and potentially high cash flow *does* exist in high growth areas, and high growth areas are now found all over Australia, in the suburbs, the regions and in the cities.

Property with good yields and potentially high cash flow does exist in high growth areas.

So, property investors need to understand that, when they buy property, it should not necessarily be with the aim of getting 'good growth' or 'good yields'. It must be for both, and the choice about *what* to buy should relate to the characteristics the property and area can show which indicates it will provide the investor with both of these things.

Having said all of that, you must know that cash flow and growth, while they can happen in the same area, rarely happen at the same time. This is because the factors which contribute to each of these events are different. Let's take a look at what those influences are.

Cash flow influences

The potential to achieve a good cash flow on a property (that is, one which is only slightly negative or, preferably positive) is impacted by a number of things, including how much access to depreciation an individual property has, an investor's own marginal rate of tax *and* the interest rates of the day. Of equal importance is the potential yield for property in an area. This will be strong, and increase, based on the following factors:

~ **A new industry or large employer coming to the area and improving employment prospects.** The result of this is that people initially move to the area for the work, and rent in that area. It takes upwards of two years for these people to become familiar enough with the area, and comfortable enough in their jobs, to consider becoming permanent residents, at which time they are likely to make a purchase decision if the area presents enough employment opportunity and community amenities.

~ **An undersupply of rentals available and so, low vacancy rates.** Usually these areas are not ready for the influx of new people and existing property feels the brunt of this sudden growth. Vacancy rates tumble and landlords are easily able to increase rents in response to this. Note that, as people often initially rent, the pressure is limited to rents, and prices at this stage most likely won't grow very much.

~ **An adjacent city or town having rents too high.** Once rents and prices grow in an adjacent city or town, people will move outward to those areas within easy commuting distance, and that area then experiences pressure on its yields. The people who do make the move to the less expensive area are more likely to initially rent, as many of them may have plans to eventually return to that original area once they can afford to do so.

Growth influences

Property value also grows as a result of a number of factors:

~ **The growth in the existing population.** This, however, will lag behind that initial boost in population which comes from migration, as migration usually impacts yields first. Population which is growing organically, as a result of people who have made ties in the areas and are starting to have families, is the kind of population growth which usually results in property prices moving higher.

~ **The increase in demand from buyers.** This is linked to many factors, including population growth and the establishment of industry. I often find that an area where small businesses are growing is an area where property prices are on the move, since the advent of more small business is a sign of intrinsic economic growth.

~ **An undersupply of property in the area.** This occurs where population is growing organically, putting pressure on existing properties;

~ **The solid establishment of diverse industry.** This is opposed to the increase in size of a single industry.

~ **An increase in migration to the area.** This could be due to improved transport and infrastructure, however this factor impacts after around two years.

~ **A vibrant local economy.** This refers to an area where the residents are becoming more affluent.

When these factors exist, people choose to settle in an area, and when they do so we see a real increase to property values which is sustainable and consistent over many years.

What should *you* pick?

Now, it may appear that I am setting up this argument to support the fact that there is a difference between cash flow and growth property, but bear with me as I explain why this knowledge is so crucial to you.

Firstly, I'll reiterate that as an investor, you will want to achieve both cash flow and growth. Cash flow allows you to hold the property as long as you need to in order to have its value increase and so add to your net worth. If your net worth doesn't grow, then a positive cash flow of $20 or so a week isn't going to do a whole lot for you in retirement. That $20 a week or so can, however, allow you to hold that property while you earn income elsewhere, and wait for the property to grow.

Conversely, while growth adds to your net worth and gives you extended options once you do retire, if the cost of that growth is too prohibitive, then you may never hold the property long enough to see it. It will be the person you are forced to sell to who might get the growth! If the cash flows are so low that you have to tip in vast quantities of your own cash to hang onto the property hoping its big growth phase arrives soon, you may lose the financial capacity to wait, and sell before time.

Let's face it, whatever you think you want from a property, all investors actually should have the goal of getting the best possible growth, and the best possible cash flow, in the period that they own the property. Each and every purchase should be made with the intent of having that property cover as much of its own costs as it can, while it has the best prognosis for growth that you can afford to support!

Even taking all of that into account, it's most unlikely that you will find properties which have a great yield, at the same time that they are on their upward growth phase. They exist of course, but to achieve that you'd have to find a property at that exact moment in time when the yields are at their maximum, right before the prices begin to rise.

You'll see from my earlier discussion that the features of an area entering its yield growth phase are factors which tend to happen at different times than those which impact on areas entering their values growth phase – they tend to happen in cycles, almost in opposition to each other.

Taking an example

When an area is in its yield growth phase, this means that the prices are remaining fairly stable, but the pressure on rents is pushing up the rent return. Here's an example.

Joanne buys a property for $200,000 with a $220 a week rent return. Her gross yield based on this price and this rent is 5.7% per annum.

Within one year, the rent increases to $280 a week. Joanne's yield has now increased to 7.2%, since it is still based upon the original price she paid for that property.

During the following year the value of the property increases to $260,000, but the rent stabilises and remains the same. Joanne's yield remains at 7.2%, since she has still only paid $200,000 and the rent topped out at $280 per week.

Joanne sells this property for $260,000 to Ben. Ben's gross yield is only 5.6%. This is because he is achieving $280 a week on his purchase price of $260,000. Joanne sold a property which was achieving a 7.2% yield for her but the new owner, Ben only saw a 5.6% yield.

To calculate yield you multiply the weekly rent by 52 to find the annual rental income. Then divide this by the purchase price. Then multiply by 100 to get the percentage. Taking Ben's yield above:

$280 x 52 = $14,460
$14,460 / $260,000 = 0.056 x 100 = 5.6%

Now, this is where the technique of buying what's just right for you comes in. Once you have identified a possible area in which to buy, you must identify which of its phases it's in. If you have found that moment in time when it's coming out of its yield phase into its growth phase, and it also has all of the criteria which make for sound investing, then grab it!

Plotting the cash flow/growth continuum

Since the above scenario is unlikely, once you have determined the phase the area is actually in, you must determine what it is you need most. To do this, you need to plot yourself on what I call the cashflow/growth continuum.

Here's an example of how to do that.

Sarah and Chris are both investors with different needs.

Sarah has considerable equity in her own home. She has owned it since before she began a family and she currently has three children, all in high school. Despite having decent paying jobs, the kids drain her and her husband of cash flow and finances are relatively tight. They can afford some negative cash flow on a property, but if they buy such a property they are most likely only able to buy one.

Sarah has the equity to add a number of properties to their portfolio, but cannot afford to do so if the properties add stress to their budget. Her immediate need is to find an area which is in its yield growth stage. She can wait for the growth phase as she is not limited by equity – only by her capacity to service the costs of more property.

Sarah would seek areas with strong indicators of a surging population, a rental undersupply and strong migration, amongst other things. It would be fine for her to add several properties in their yield growth phase, as long as those properties have the potential to reach a values growth phase soon enough.

Remember, buying for cash flow alone is not suitable. An investor must buy for cash flow in an area with the signs that growth will occur at some stage during their period of ownership.

Chris has very little equity. He lives in his principal place of residence which he hasn't owned long and in which he has not had the time to build up equity. Chris has no dependants and is single, with a well paying job and high personal cash flows. While he has the cash flow to support many properties, he is limited by his equity and the speed with which he can save deposits.

For Chris, the prime objective is to buy property which is in its values growth phase – if the yield is slightly low, he can most likely afford to hang on to the property and supplement the cash flow from his own funds, as he has the available personal cash flow to do this. As the property is growing, the commitment of these funds is rewarded with a growth to the capital value.

Buyers of property like this must be sure they have done the research which clearly indicates every chance for good growth.

As Chris buys property in its growth phase he is likely to build equity more quickly so that, if he reaches the limits of his available personal cash flow, he can then begin to buy property in its yield growth phase, where less personal cash input is required. Equally, once Sarah has a number of properties in her portfolio and her cash flow is stronger, she can start to look at buying property in its growth phase to once again boost that equity she has been using.

The process

As an investor, you must first work out what you need, at the exact time you are buying. Are you at the point in your investing life where cash flow is of prime importance or is it growth you need? Maybe you can buy one or two properties with growth, then one or two with cash flow, and so on. You must plot yourself on the yield/growth continuum and be guided by those needs when it comes to area selection.

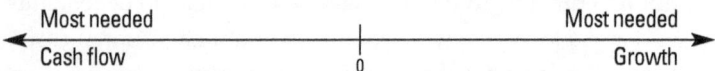

Most needed Cash flow ←——————|——————→ Most needed Growth

0

I have 20 Questions® that firstly narrow down those areas which have the best prognosis for investing success, and then eliminate those areas which cannot satisfy your immediate need for either cash flow or growth. These 20 Questions® are discussed in detail in my book, *20 Must Ask Questions for Every Property Investor* (published by Wiley).

Chapter 5 will help you to conduct thorough due diligence in your property search. As you carry out this due diligence, you will pop areas onto your list which are from both the regions and from the cities, that have either a strong yield or strong growth prognosis. Your ultimate selection must not rely upon whether it's a city-based or country-based property, the price, or whether it's favoured by others, or whether you've read about it being a hotspot. Your selection must be due to the area's ability to ultimately deliver both cash flow and growth during the period you own it, and your own needs right at this time as to which is most important to you to occur first.

The investor's responsibility

I hope that by now you can see that being an investor carries a huge responsibility. Every day I receive email from people who are looking for the quick answer – someone to buy property for them, the short-cut to investing in property or ways to eliminate the hard work. I also get more than my fair share of email from people who have tried to buy the quick route by engaging self-proclaimed experts who either sell them property which is wrong for them, or don't deliver the right kind of guidance. I've been told of those who spend $15,000 on mentoring, only to find that after one year they still have not moved off first base. Others tell of buying property in areas which never stacked up, and being left holding properties worth less than they paid with no chance of strong yields or a resale any time soon.

The only real way to become a little more protected against making an investment which doesn't turn out well is to become educated and do the hard yards on your own. Keep abreast of the latest investing information and fully understand what drives growth, which features make one area perform when another seemingly similar area fails. If an adviser you are taking counsel from is still hawking the same message they have done for years, ask them why, or better still find someone else to guide you. Our changing economy ultimately has a big impact on how property behaves, and becoming aware of how economic influences eventually impact on property is a crucial part of your own education.

Above all take your time and choose property with a calm head, devoid of the emotion which creates the mistakes in the first place. I'd suggest that 80% of errors made by property investors relate in some way back to their emotions, or a misplaced sense that they in some way have an instinct for buying property.

There is no such thing as instinct and no substitution for the often tedious, hard work of gathering facts, checking information and researching the area thoroughly. Do this and you will reduce your risk factor tenfold, and likely end up with a sound portfolio of properties which provide all the lifestyle benefits you're hoping for.

Now, the nitty gritty!

By now you should have plotted yourself on that continuum and become aware of just what it is you need most in the next property you buy. You should also have a fair idea of the areas which are potentially right, and those which you shouldn't waste your time upon.

This means that you are now ready to more thoroughly explore those areas to decide whether they are right for you, or not, and whether they have the potential to really achieve hotspot status. The hard work now begins!

KEY POINTS

~ The days are gone where city living is the preference.

~ Industry and business is relocating and decentralising.

~ Negative gearing and positive gearing are tax terms, *not* strategies.

~ Some areas will have cash flow *and* growth and others will have neither.

~ Cash flow and values growth rarely occur simultaneously.

~ Investors must work out which they need *first* and buy in those areas entering that phase in its cash flow/values growth cycle.

DUE DILIGENCE AND MY 20 MUST ASK QUESTIONS®

We've examined how property ultimately delivers the return to you which helps you to become financially secure and make choices about when, and how well, you can retire. In some ways the information from the prior chapter was a little out of place, since the process of establishing what phase of the yield/growth cycle an area is at should occur *after* you have found the area!

However, it was important to understand the dynamics of how yield and growth operate as two prime parts of a successful investment whole, and that was my reasoning behind including it early in this book. From here I'd like to take a backward step, as it were, and look at how to actually choose property using a range of criteria that ensure you complete the best, most exhaustive due diligence. These criteria are essentially drawn from the economic overlay which you should use when investing in property, and which I discussed in detail in Chapter 3.

The due diligence I always employ before I purchase investment property is structured around my 20 Questions®.

These questions need to be answered before you take action. So successful is this approach that these questions have been stolen, copied, reworked and disguised, and because of that I'd say they really contain ground-breaking information. People don't steal bad ideas, do they?

I created this list of questions based on personal experiences and an investing history which had spanned the 10 years prior to writing them. I retrospectively examined my own substantial portfolio to establish exactly what made some of my properties such winners, and others only lukewarm investments. The resulting 20 Questions® then became the basis upon which I have enhanced my own knowledge, by exploring economic influences and establishing that overall economic landscape against which these questions can be posed.

You may have read my book *The 20 Must Ask Questions®* *for Every Property Investor* (published by Wiley). It's a comprehensive analysis of my 20 Questions®, how to ask them, who might answer them and the answers they may elicit. If you haven't already done so, I suggest you seek out *The 20 Must Ask Questions® for Every Property Investor* (published by Wiley). That book will become your bible for all investment property purchasing transactions, and you will find that you use it again and again with each new purchase.

In all of my books I like to offer fresh, new information, and so I won't provide the questions again here in detail. Instead, in this chapter I discuss the broad areas within which your due diligence must fall for any property you are considering. Broadly, there are four areas your research and questioning should attempt to address:

1. Factors affecting the property's financials
2. Information about the area's economics
3. Factors impacting upon the property and its returns
4. Your personal circumstances (not including the cash flows, which make up the property's financials).

The Property's Financials

The financials of a property comprise factors that impact upon your personal income and expenses, those with which the bank is concerned, and those which relate to the actual value of the property.

Those impacting upon you

In any of my books you will find a comprehensive discussion about cash flows. You can almost track the history of how property in Australia has performed by reading these past books. When I began writing, yields on property in many parts of the country were quite exceptional and interest rates were fairly low, meaning that many areas had the potential to have a positive cash flow (remember, this means raw rent return is greater than raw expenses, or it could also mean that after-tax income is greater than after-tax costs). Since some of those areas also possessed intrinsic growth drivers, then to be a successful investor it made no sense to do anything other than look for positive cash flow property.

Some years later, property values had grown in many parts of the country, and rent returns had remained stable. Interest rates had risen too, which made it much harder to see a positive cash flow of any description. At that time, I recommended buying property which showed signs that rent returns were about to come under pressure, even if that meant experiencing a negative cash flow in the short term.

To meet that negative cash flow an investor had to be disciplined and willing to make budget cuts until such times as the cash flow improved.

In today's market (late 2011), we are seeing a variety of cash flow outcomes, depending upon exactly where the area is in its cycle, and what we expect to occur next – a growth in value or a growth in rental yield. Remember, as previously explained, some areas will experience both, some one or the other, and some neither.

...some areas will experience both (growth and yield), some one or the other, and some neither.

When looking at the property financials, you must consider the area's capacity to achieve both cash flow and growth, and your own needs *at that time*.

At this point you should have determined just which of the two outcomes is most important to you. You should have also considered whether the area you are currently examining can deliver both cash flow and growth at some time.

The next step is to determine the most likely purchase price and the most likely rent return of a property in that area, and then carry out some calculations to determine what a likely cash flow may be. To do this, you must also assess potential costs and potential on-paper deductions, such as depreciation. Since this can be difficult for the novice we have provided free software with the purchase of this book which can provide 'rule of thumb' calculations for you. Details of how to obtain the software can be found at the back of this book.

Once you have done these calculations you will be in a position to determine if you can actually afford the after-tax costs of buying an investment property in that area.

Factors with which the bank is concerned

I am not going to outline all of the different ways that you can finance a property strategy, since my book *How to Create an Income for Life* (published by Wiley) contains comprehensive information about how to do this. Having said that, the correct finance structure is a vital component of your investment strategy, and if this is not established at the outset, it can be costly in terms of lost taxation advantages and even involve significant costs to re-do if that becomes necessary.

An important factor to consider is that not all lenders will advance funds to buy any property, in any area. Some of the major lenders have minimum population criteria before they will lend for a purchase, which is normally in the vicinity of 5,000 to 7,000 people.

If you want to borrow to buy a residential property which is in an area with a population greater than that, you can usually borrow up to 90% or even 95% of the value of that property. Of course, if you do borrow more than 80%, you may have to pay Lender's Mortgage Insurance, which is a policy put in place to meet any shortfall between sale price and the outstanding loan should the bank have to foreclose.

Another factor that a bank will consider carefully is the 'purpose' of the property (see later section on Property Use). Niche market property generally has specific rules, and each lender has a different approach to how they finance these properties. Be sure you are familiar with them before committing to buy one.

Factors which affect the market value

In order for you to build equity as quickly as possible on any property you buy, you need to ensure that when you buy it you have purchased at a reasonable market value. Market value of one property isn't determined by the listed price of the properties around it, or by the listed price of houses similar to one you may be looking at. In short, 'market value' can otherwise be expressed as 'what the market is prepared to pay', and recent *sale* prices are the best indication of this.

As I write this book I am negotiating on my next property. I have found something just right and assessed its market value at \$220,000. The owners are refusing to accept anything below \$230,000. It's exceptionally hard for me to walk away from this one, and some would say that it is only \$10,000, but that will then be \$10,000 more that I have to recover, since it's likely that other similar properties will sell at closer to true market value. Since I am sure of my facts, I must be strong and stick to my decision, and despite having a bit of an emotional connection to this one property, I'm not budging.

> 'Market value' can otherwise be expressed as 'what the market is prepared to pay'.

The greatest problem buying a property at over market value becomes evident during a slowdown in the market. If the market stalls just after you have bought a property, and you have paid over market value, your property will quickly lose value and, if an unforseen circumstance occurs and you have to sell, you can experience real loss. Over the years the risk that paying over market value presents tends to diminish as the market value grows.

Always do remember that the list price is not market value. Vendors always ask for more than they want, and the result is that many buyers often pay more than they need to! Always verify your facts by using an online data source, or the local agent's knowledge to discover the value of recent sales in the area.

The area's economics

Throughout this book I've referred to the significant role of micro economics in the ability of any area to perform consistently and sustainably, so that you buy in an area which has its best performance just after you buy there. Generally speaking, there are many factors which relate to the area's economics and I have so far covered them in detail. Following is more specific information about those characteristics.

Economic growth

Earlier in this book I discussed economic growth and the macro economic influences which ultimately translate into property growth. In addition to examining those broader economic influences, you must consider the micro economic factors which create a local economy that is either in sync with the nation, or behaving counter-cyclically. Remember that it is highly possible for an area to be experiencing an economic upswing in the face of a nation's downswing, and if this is the case, a hotspot is most likely in the making.

It is highly possible for an area to be experiencing an economic upswing in the face of a nation's downswing.

In addition to that, as a property investor you should be looking for property *all* of the time, not just when property investing seems to be favoured by the economy and by other investors. To that end, there are a number of things to be looking out for in the areas where you are concentrating your search which can give useful hints about economic vibrancy. They are:

~ *An increasing median household income.* Household income increasing at a faster rate than inflation indicates that the local population is becoming more affluent, and in turn is likely to be spending money back in the area. This is not the case where the population consists mainly of fly in/fly out workers, who usually spend money in their home town, and the areas where they are working are typically economically unstable.

~ *The diversification of industry within the area.* Large companies relocating, especially where they are of an industry type that had not previously existed in the area, draw workers from a different pool.

~ *Lower commercial vacancy rates.* Commercial vacancies reducing give an indication that small business is becoming more vibrant.

~ *The building of new shopping malls.* The large companies that undertake these building projects usually research extensively into future consumer demand before they commit to such investment and you can piggy-back off this research.

~ *Upgraders.* If the majority of property purchases are being made by existing residents upgrading this is further proof that the area and its occupants are becoming more economically vibrant.

~ *Abundant new infrastructure planning.* There is a big difference between upgrading existing infrastructure and building all new projects, such as railway lines and new roads. Local government rarely makes such large commitments without evidence of strong underlying economic vibrancy.

~ *Tenure of residents.* The longer the tenants generally stay in an area, the more probability that the area will grow. This tenure then extends to subsequent generations, who are more likely to remain in an area where they have relatives.

~ *Jobs growth.* This leads to a lowering of the unemployment rate.

Remember, this is a micro search you are carrying out – the overall economy of the nation could be showing a different reading, while the local economy may well be bucking the trend.

Population data

We already know that the population of the country is growing, both through increasing birth-rates and through immigration. A growing population ultimately impacts on demand for property, but generally speaking the current rate of population will most likely only affect property values at the same rate as inflation. Therefore, it's not enough to simply confirm that an area you are interested in has a population which is growing, although indeed you do not want to be buying in an area that has a population which is shrinking. Rather, it is important that you seek out areas where the population is growing faster than the national average.

If a large population exists in an area, this is not a reason to believe that it is also an area which will naturally grow and put pressure on prices. This is one of the reasons why many established areas where property is held for the long term, and where people may aspire to live, fail to achieve the property price growth which is often a feature of smaller, underdeveloped areas.

Once population reaches a certain level, unless some big 'kicker' exists to increase population and so increase demand for property in the area, the area will become one of those I previously referred to as offering stable growth only, rather than better than average growth.

If you can remember at all times that you are looking for an area which will have its greatest period of growth just after you buy it, and after that growth occurs it will settle into stable growth, you will see the importance of this population information.

Population needs to be, in the first instance, large enough to result in organic population growth – that is, growth happening from within as well as growth occurring from migration to the area – and in the second instance growing faster than the national average. This growth should be occurring across all age demographics, not just within one demographic group, as a community needs a good spread of ages to secure tenure of residents.

Support for that population growth

Where the population is growing, local government needs to be involved in significant planning and development in order to provide for the continuing and sometimes changing needs of that population.

When a new, or not long established, area begins to grow and prosper, much of the infrastructure we expect to service an area may not initially be provided. Generally speaking, housing developments commence and exist before adequate services, such as shopping centres, schools and transport are provided by local government.

Equally, where a more established area which previously catered for a smaller population is now growing organically as a result of improved employment opportunities, many of the typical upgrades required to underpin strong population growth are yet to occur. These include road upgrades, curb and guttering, community centres, etc.

It's possible for an area to have great potential to grow into a thriving community, but if this population growth is not, at some time, underpinned by the provision of adequate services, the population is likely to reach a critical mass, and then grow no further.

Those local governments which recognise this and continually fight for the funds to provide the services their communities require build areas which continue to grow, year in and year out. Examining the infrastructure plans which have been put in place by the council, where funds exist to bring them to fruition, is an important part of your research.

Population spread

Property investment 'experts' often claim that you must buy in the CBD, or at least in a large capital city, in order to access the best rates of growth. I have already smashed this myth earlier in the book and shown how the opposite can in fact be true.

I will never suggest that an area needs to be near a capital city in order for it to be viable – many areas which make for great investing aren't anywhere near a capital city. The point is that sometimes a smaller area, or outer suburb which does not have many of its own growth drivers, may still enjoy some growth because of the wave effect of the close, larger and more vibrant area and the population grows and begins to spread. Where that larger area, which may have already experienced some great growth, is enjoying very low vacancy rates and rents are skyrocketing, smaller adjacent areas or towns will often benefit from the flow-on effect, as long as they are within commutable distance of the larger area.

This is *not* an excuse to buy property in that small country town you like the look of, or the little place where you were born! But it is food for thought and a suggestion that you consider any smaller areas which may be within half an hour or so of the bigger area which has had a recent boom. There is plenty of support for this strategy at the moment – so many of our outer suburbs and larger regional towns are experiencing growth which is far better than their close large cities.

Population types

Knowing who lives in an area, and if this is changing, has an influence upon property choice. The question I am most often asked is, 'should I buy a unit or a house?'

A close examination of the age demographic and the industry types will provide useful hints as to what to buy. In some areas, units are more in demand and so this property type grows faster. In others, typically those with high concentrations of families, houses are favoured and so grow in value better, usually achieving higher yields along the way. An understanding of the types of people living in an area, and the likelihood that this will remain constant, is vital when choosing a property type which will perform well over the longer term.

Employment factors

Where an area exists for the purposes of servicing one major industry, you are taking on a greater risk buying property in that location. While investors certainly can, and do, experience significant growth in both yields and value when they purchase in a mining area, they must be aware of the significance of the added risk.

When the GFC hit, it was virtually unexpected and certainly not forecast by most economists. A detailed examination of the global economy may have pointed to a probable economic downswing, however the actual fallout was greater than could have been imagined, let alone predicted. In reality, that economically cataclysmic event was triggered by some bad decisions made at local levels in one country, and the butterfly effect quickly echoed and magnified the final result.

Equally, investing in a town based solely on only one industry carries a risk far greater than buying property in an area where the industry is diversified. An event which may initially have little to do with that one industry may eventually develop to create an impact great enough to negatively affect the fortunes of that industry. Where an entire area relies upon that one industry, and its related industries (such as retail and hospitality) for its income, a closure of that industry can have swift and devastating effects upon those who own property. An investor may go quickly from having a property with a high value and exceptional rental returns to one with no tenant, and no buyers.

Investing in a town based solely on only one industry carries a risk far greater.

I'll never argue that significant gains can be made by those who invest in towns such as these, typically mining towns. However, all investing must be undertaken with a sound grasp of the true risks involved. If you are prepared to accept those risks, and you have considered what your position would be if you owned a property that suffered a significant loss, then a one-industry town may be an excellent investment for you. If you need a little more surety in your investing, stick with areas offering more diversity, which can manage industry closures because there are many other employers to take up the slack.

The property and its returns

Trend analysis

If you have ever invested in shares, you may well be familiar with the technique of buying according to 'technical analysis' research. An investor using technical analysis to choose shares will look at the historical performance of a share and the sharemarket, and attempt to forecast a future performance based on that alone. The intrinsic value of the share, which relates to the health and potential of the company itself, is not considered in technical analysis.

As you have already learned from this book, the intrinsic value of an area is the most vital component of your research and to continue the comparison with the sharemarket, it is akin to 'fundamental analysis'. Examining in detail what is likely to happen in the future, in combination with the current economic vibrancy of an area, will go a long way toward ensuring that you choose an area with every chance of exceeding the average property performance at that time, and improving on the result you may have had if you had invested in another asset class.

Having said that, some trends can give you added information by which you can measure this intrinsic potential. They are as follows.

Price growth trends

If you are hearing about great growth in any one area, find out what's driving that growth. Extrinsic growth drivers bring short-term, unsustainable growth while intrinsic drivers deliver the opposite – sustainable growth (see more about this in the next chapter). If extrinsic growth drivers are creating the growth you are seeing, it may be a false reading on growth and so may not be an area in which to buy.

You should also explore the growth figures from the past few years. Strong growth for several years often ends in a slowdown *unless* additional drivers, such as plans for improvement to transport links, still exist.

If, on the other hand, an area has had low growth for the past five years, but still seems to have a growing population, take a closer look. You should find out what is causing that population growth because if it is occurring as a result of permanent employment arising from new industry in town, you may be just ahead of a turnaround in these growth figures.

Vacancy rates and rental income trends

There are some great online tools which exist to help you to establish rent trends. One in particular can be found at www.sqmresearch.com.au. Here you can see not only the current vacancy rates of an area, but the trend of vacancies over the prior two years. This is a good stepping off point for establishing rent trends – a downward trending vacancy rate usually results in increasing rents, and vice versa.

It's useful also to have a chat with a local property manager to discover what is happening with rents in the area. Find out if rents have been going up, staying the same or falling. Increasing rents are always good news, unless the increase occurred as a result of short-term demand from the workers on a large infrastructure project which is now complete for example, or from a large industry which has ceased operation.

Increasing rents are always good news, unless the increase occurred as a result of short-term demand.

Analysing those trends

You must bear in mind that the trends discussed here are the barometers that you can use to determine what will happen next. As I have said earlier in this book, these trends must be considered in concert with all of the other information you are obtaining. Here is how you read the potential trends.

~ *Rental yield growth alone* – Where the yields that you can obtain on properties in that area seem to have grown, while the values have remained stable, several things may be at play. Ask about whether there has recently been a large project completed, the construction of which required the employment of itinerant workers. If new industry has come to town, confirm its permanency and success, as this may indicate even more rental growth to come.

~ *Price growth alone* – Sometimes demand for property in an area comes all at once due to a number of factors. This can result in frenzied buying and we see prices increasing suddenly, with auctions well attended and people paying well over the reserve price to secure what they see as being a scarce commodity. Where you have established that price growth has trended up more recently, find out what is driving this. Again you want to be sure that the factors driving the prices up are lasting and likely to continue. Sometimes, the short-term rental demand creates a false impression of the demand for property in the area and investors rush in to take advantage of this rental yield increase, wanting to get in on the ground floor of a positive cash flow property. This sudden interest can be the very thing which pushes up the price and, once the rental demand eases and rents begin to drop, prices will follow as distressed landlords try to quickly liquidate their investments.

~ *When you can't achieve either one!* – Just because an area shows neither growing property prices nor growing rent returns does not automatically exclude it from your consideration. You may find that all the other research covered in this chapter is met with a positive outcome, but there has not yet been a rent increase or a price increase. In this situation, I'd suggest that the area may be an undiscovered gem, and you may well be one of the lucky few who buy before the masses do.

Supply factors

Earlier I discussed the importance of being aware of population trends so that you can make some viable judgements about future demand for your property. It's important to realise that you will have a relatively fixed pool of tenants, albeit a potentially increasing one, and while you may have ascertained that the supply of tenants is on the rise, you also need to ascertain if the supply of options for those tenants is also increasing.

Discovering what future land releases the council intends to allow can assist you to determine ahead of time if you are likely to face increased competition. Asking what current development applications have been lodged will help further narrow this down into potential competition in the area directly around where you are buying.

Owning a property which is most in demand is crucial, but if that demand is watered down when more of the exact same property that you own is built and sold, you may struggle to attract a tenant, and this will have the flow-on effect of reducing your yield as you are forced to lower rents to compete with others.

Property use

The term 'niche market, or 'special-use property' is applied to any property which has been purpose-built to cater to a specific market. Such property is generally built with an exact market in mind and as such it is often of a design which is different from standard residential property. Sometimes an existing residential property may be altered to suit a specific category, for example where a house has been modified to house a number of individual university students who don't have a pre-existing relationship.

You will know a niche market property when you see one, and often they are heavily marketed on the basis of a perceived added value or increased chance of better yields. All too often these better yields don't materialise, and very often the value of the property is impacted negatively because it is niche market.

The kinds of niche market properties which are typically seen today are described below.

Multi-resident accommodation

This refers to any kind of property which has been built or modified in order to attract a number of tenants who do not have a pre-existing relationship. This type of property is becoming more popular in mining towns, targeting fly in/fly out workers, and in university towns or suburbs where students reside during the academic semester. Tenants are quite itinerant and come with additional issues which you must consider.

Specific demographic options

Such a term refers to any property built to target a specific age demographic. These include:

~ *Retirement accommodation* – In many states retirement properties may only be owned by the resident. Some also cannot be rented out. However, in some states we have seen the emergence of 'over 55s' accommodation. Typically these are small units built in a complex which may provide activities especially for people over 55, yet they are not retirement villages or aged care facilities as no level of care is offered.

~ *Student accommodation* (also mentioned above) – is built usually near universities and specifically designed to house a number of unrelated students in the one building.

~ *Hotel accommodation* – comprises hotels, serviced apartments, holiday houses and even time-share arrangements built for the tourist. Some of them have what is known as 'pooled income', where the income from the entire property is pooled and then equally distributed – regardless of whether your unit had tenants – and others are let individually. A whole host of management arrangements also exist which further add to the risk of these property types.

There are two crucial issues to consider when buying such property. Firstly, regardless of the use, the underlying asset must qualify as a sound investment. If such properties are built in areas which do *not* qualify as economically vibrant, then they should not be considered. Your job is to find a suitable area *first* and then decide later what kind of property best fits the demand which exists there. Sadly, where niche market property is concerned, investors are normally attracted by the property type first, assessing the potential success of the purchase purely against its attractiveness as a hotel, aged-care facility or student residence. In doing so, many such investors typically ignore whether the property has actually been built in an area which satisfies the due diligence covered here and my 20 Must Ask Questions®.

> Regardless of the use, the underlying asset must qualify as a sound investment.

The second issue to consider is whether or not the property can be repurposed. If the original intent for the property fails for some reason, you need to be sure that there is a second end-use for that niche market property. You must also ensure that, if you plan at some time in the future to repurpose such a property, your plans to do so will be acceptable at council level.

Who is building?

In most cases, property investors buy established properties. At times, they instead buy a property recently built, or one which has been sold off-the-plan with a finish date some years down the track.

You may be looking at a property which is quite new. If it is less than six years old it will more than likely come with a current builder's warranty, which has value to you because if you find any defects in the property during the period covered by the warranty they must be fixed by the builder, and this will save you money.

If you are building a new property, get to know the builder. While it's easy enough to go along to a display village, it's more important to actually be able to speak to someone who has previously retained the builder's services, and, if possible, to look at a finished product which is not in a display village. Builders should be happy to provide you with referrals to happy clients, if they have them!

Buying off-the-plan is more complex, because you are locked into a contract sometimes even before the soil has even been turned. You won't get the chance to view anything other than a plan and will have to trust the builder and developer to deliver on their promise. Such contracts are usually water-tight for the vendor but not so for the buyer, and the vendor often includes fine print allowing them to rescind the contract for a range of reasons. Discover if the developer has been involved in other successful projects and take a look at them. Speak to owners if possible.

While developers have to guarantee sound building work, they are not usually carrying out the actual work themselves and you will want to know whether they have chosen a quality builder with a good track record before you proceed.

The property itself

It's likely (in fact often preferable) that you will not personally view a property before you buy. If you intend to buy widely and in the best possible area at the time you are ready to buy, then it's most unlikely that the area will just happen to be where you live, or even be within driving distance of your house!

You still need to be sure that the condition of the property is acceptable, which is why this research is important. If the property is not habitable for some reason, you may need to spend money on repairs to make it so. If you have not planned this in your budget, it can add considerably to your buying costs and impact on your subsequent cash flow. It is acceptable to buy a property in need of repair, as long as you are aware of what these repairs entail, and account for their costs in your initial calculations. Sometimes such repair work can be a useful bargaining tool!

> It's likely (in fact often preferable) that you will not personally view a property before you buy.

You don't have to inspect the property to ascertain its condition. If you are anything like me, an inspection will only make it harder to reject a property that you fall in love with, or worse, result in you rejecting a perfectly good investment on the basis of your personal feelings about it. However, someone should look at it, and rather than spend money paying for inspections on property you have not decided to buy as yet, you can use the services of a willing property manager. A manager who is interested in obtaining your business will almost certainly carry out a habitability inspection before you buy, if asked.

Earlier in this book I referred to the impact that on-paper claims can have on your cash flow. A property does not have to be newer or even eligible for on-paper claims to make it a viable investment. However, when it comes to property selection, if you are choosing between two similar properties with two similar rent returns and purchase prices, the one which is newer will provide better cash flows from on-paper claims.

As well as the actual condition of the property, you should be considering its hardiness. For a property which you will live in yourself, it's nice to have all the mod cons and expensive fixtures and fittings. When choosing an investment property you have to consider whether the property is going to require costly upkeep, as this will impact directly on your return. Low-cost fixtures and fittings, little in the way of gardens and easy-care floor coverings are a must if you intend to keep costs to a minimum.

It's also important to take out a 'Landlord's Insurance' policy. Holding landlord's insurance will not make a property more tenant-friendly, but it may assist with repair costs in the event that anything in your property is damaged by your tenants.

Your personal circumstances

Considering a range of factors which may affect your personal circumstances, either upon buying a property or while you are holding it, becomes the next vital step in your due diligence. There are several considerations which need to be made, as follows:

Risk

One of the things which amazes me the most about many property investors is that they fail to acknowledge or examine the sometimes significant risks which exist when making any investment. This is most likely because many property investors are what I call 'accidental investors'; the decision to invest has been arrived at after the opportunity to purchase a property has been presented to them. They may have noticed that the property down the road was on the market, or been given a brochure which advertised a great investment opportunity, and so the decision was made to buy.

> Many property investors are what I call 'accidental investors'; the decision to invest has been arrived at after the opportunity to purchase a property has been presented to them.

Investors in any other type of financial product will generally be required to complete a risk profile and establish the right type of investment to match their financial goals before they proceed, but this rarely occurs within the property industry, where risk is seldom addressed.

The property investment industry is currently not regulated in any way, and I explore that issue later in this book. Because of this there is no 'best practice' when it comes to selling property to an investor or advising them how to buy it, and no compliance to any law required. This increases the risk that you will buy something not right for you – if the adviser isn't finding out your appetite for risk via a risk profile assessment, there is a greater likelihood you will buy the wrong property and not achieve the results for which you were hoping.

Property investors need to consider risk in two ways: firstly they must understand their attitude to risk, so that they can establish the degree to which they should leverage, how quickly they should buy, and if indeed property suits their goals at all. Then, they must be familiar with the risk rating of the different *types* of property, so that they can buy property which matches their own, personal risk profile.

Later in this book I more thoroughly explore the extent of risk which applies to property investors, and the different kinds of risk that may exist. In my book *The 20 Must Ask Questions® for Every Property Investor* (published by Wiley) I have provided a complete analysis of each different property type and applied a risk rating to assist you to decide if it matches your personal risk profile.

Rent guarantees, tax schemes and other incentives

You may come across a property where the developer offers an incentive such as a rent guarantee. This means that there is an agreement in place promising some form of assured rent return. It may be that the seller of the property tops up actual rent received to a pre-agreed amount, or covers the weekly rental payment if no tenant is in place.

This promise is not really a 'free lunch' – often properties with such a guarantee cost more, because the guarantee has been built into the price.

The guarantee refers to the amount of rent that is to be received. It is not a guarantee that the property will be rented, and this is an important distinction to make. A rent guarantee only guarantees that:

~ you will receive regular weekly or monthly rent;
~ that rent will be a pre-agreed amount; and

~ the rent will be paid for a pre-agreed term.

It does *not* guarantee:

~ the tenant is paying the promised amount, and so it may actually be unachievable;

~ a tenant will always be in the property;

~ the tenant will remain after the rent guarantee period is over, or pay a higher amount once it is over;

~ the property is built in an area presenting the best investment opportunity at that moment in time.

To be honest, a rent guarantee does not always even guarantee those first three things – I've seen many of them fall over when the entity offering that guarantee goes out of business, and there is little the property owner can do to recover any funds lost as a result.

A rent guarantee won't transform an investment which has other inherent problems like shoddy building work, or having been built in the worst part of town. I am always quite suspicious of any property with a rent guarantee. All of the properties I have ever bought have been purchased because they satisfy my 20 Questions®, and because I have done such extensive research that I confirm a demand for the property and find evidence that the area is growing and prospering. I don't need a rent guarantee to push me over the line, and the proof that I have chosen well is in the form of a continuing and suitable income stream. If there is a rent guarantee I have to enquire what is wrong with that property – why can't it stand on its own two feet?

Of course if you do find a property with a guaranteed rent in an area which does satisfy each and every one of my

20 Must Ask Questions® and all your other due diligence, it's like having a little bit of icing on an already delicious cake!

I am often asked about seemingly government-backed guarantees such as Defence Force Housing and the National Rental Affordability Scheme (NRAS). Defence housing is an example of a rent guarantee which includes all of the management costs in return for guaranteeing a tenant, while the NRAS involves significant tax advantages for buying property which is rented to disadvantaged tenants for 20% below the market rent. There are others, and I am sure over the years more will be offered.

As with all such incentives, the overlying 'scheme of arrangement' cannot change the value, or otherwise, of the underlying investment.

After purchase management

If you are purchasing a residential house or unit, it is most likely that it will be managed by either you, or by a property manager. Niche market properties can come with a range of other options which can intensify your risks, and so knowing beforehand what kind of management is likely to be in place is a crucial part of the process. It's not straightforward and there are a number of potential arrangements which may either be in place before you buy, or be on offer to you after you buy.

A standard residential house or unit will be either self-managed by you, the owner, or professionally managed by a professional property management company.

There are a lot of things which must be done when a property is managed. They include, but are not limited to:

~ advertising the property on professional websites to attract a tenant;

~ carrying out background checks on potential tenants to be sure they have a clean rental history;

~ drawing up a fair lease which protects the tenant's and the landlord's rights;

~ collecting the rent and acquitting it to the owner;

~ following up on tenant requests;

~ arranging for handymen and other tradesmen when repair work is needed;

~ attending court if there are any disputes or non-payment of rent or breaking any conditions of the lease;

~ answering tenant enquiries.

If you believe you have the skills, networks and contacts to carry out this job smoothly and cost-effectively, then you might consider self-management.

If however, like me, you believe you are a property investor, not a property manager, you should leave this very important job to the experts. The cost of experienced property management is minute in comparison to the actual work required, and this cost is tax-deductible.

The agreement you have with a property manager will be expressed in a legal management agreement which, while in a printed form, can be changed to suit both parties. Don't be fooled into thinking that just because the agreement is in black and white its terms are concrete – you can ask for any changes you like, and it will be up to the manager to decide if they agree to that change or not. Like all contracts, these are negotiable.

Non-standard residential property

Earlier in this chapter we considered a range of niche market property options. Generally speaking, niche market property will have its own unique style of management, often under an agreement which is not the same as a standard property management agreement.

The property which you have found may have an onsite caretaker or manager, a professional hotel group leasing out rooms to travellers, or a new kind of management with which you may not be familiar. Some of these arrangements involve the handing over of many rights you might have as a landlord, and others may involve a third-party running a business, such as a holiday letting service, in your property.

The cost of experienced property management is minute in comparison to the actual work required, and this cost is tax-deductible.

This of course will make the ongoing management of your investment much more complex, and add risk to the investment. The risk might be limited to some kind of property damage, or it could be as great as the entire venture failing, impacting directly upon your capacity to obtain an income.

If you are thinking of buying any property which falls outside of the confines of regular property management, be sure that you seek legal advice as to your rights and responsibilities.

Are you emotionally involved?

I have seen property investors go to an amazing amount of trouble with their research, only to make a bad choice in the end, or to follow their 'gut feeling' and buy something they felt good about instead. Glossy brochures and snappy salesmen can work against your better judgement, and before the ink is dry on your contract, you may begin to regret your decision.

If you promise yourself that you will remain unemotional, and you follow the guidelines I have set in this book, you will have a sound and logical basis upon which to make a purchase decision. By using the data you collect, rather than viewing a property and making a decision based on gut-feeling, you will put space between you and the decision, and be more likely to consider all aspects of that investment.

If you commit to not only thoroughly carrying out appropriate due diligence, but to being guided by the information you uncover, you will reduce your chances of buying a bad investment tenfold. This process of thorough research may not guarantee that you buy the best ever investment, but I believe it will go a long way toward protecting you from buying the worst ever investment!

If you've gone to the trouble of reading to here, it's just as important that you get hold of a copy of my 20 Questions® book when you are ready to make an actual purchase. If you want to get it right, be sure to be guided by that book as you go through the process of researching your next purchase.

KEY POINTS

1. Your due diligence should comprise researching a number of factors that affect the property's financials. You need to find answers to a number of questions to put your own mind at rest and also to satisfy your lender.

2. Find out about the economics of the area where you are considering investing investing – what are its growth prospects, the population and employment trends of the town, suburb or region?

3. Look carefully at the property itself and don't let there be any surprises waiting for you after purchase. You need to uncover any factors impacting upon the property and its returns before you buy.

4. Due diligence should also cover a review of your own personal circumstances, including your tolerance for risk and how it varies depending on the type of property investment you make.

6

GROWTH DRIVERS

We've been taking a pretty complex journey through the landscape of property investing. Hopefully, I have helped you to see that a range of influences must work critically together to produce an area which is most likely to become a hotspot.

You certainly can't get this right every time, and it's definitely not an exact science. However, I do think that a good feel for the broader economic landscape, when considered alongside facts and features about an area, will go a long way toward helping you to make really good choices about property, rarely getting it too wrong.

In all of my seminars, when I am hosting one of my TV shows, and writing articles and even new books, I consistently refer to growth drivers. In a sense, growth drivers refer to many of the things which I have already discussed in this book, and they are definitely related to the micro-economy of an area.

While I don't want to rehash what has already been said

here in this book, I do want to discuss all of these drivers to show you how some drivers point to future and sustained growth, while others may point to temporary and unsustainable growth. It's almost as if some growth drivers are in disguise, and may trick you into believing an area has more going for it than it really does.

What is a growth driver?

You may be reading this and thinking that this is a silly question, since all we have really talked about so far is growth and those factors which impact positively on both yield growth and values growth.

Here I would like to cover the important differences between those drivers which exist within an area, and those which create growth by occurring outside of an area. It is important to make this distinction since those occurring within an area will have a far more positive impact on the performance of your investment than those which are considered to be external influences. By being able to place the economic data you are reading into one of these two separate groups, you will be able to make a stronger prediction about the future potential of that area.

Extrinsic growth drivers

As the name suggests, extrinsic growth drivers are the economic influences which contribute to the growth of an area, but which originate outside of that area. They are not a result of any micro economic changes within that area, but do come from activity, planning and events which occur temporarily.

When a large infrastructure project or a major building project is planned and executed in an area which has a smaller population, there is generally insufficient local labour available to fill the jobs which are being created. Often, workers will come from surrounding areas, or even from interstate, and for the period of the project, they will be living in that area, most likely in rental accommodation.

This will place a temporary pressure on many of those economic factors which you will be looking at. The retail and hospitality trade will improve as these new residents spend what they are earning, back into the local economy. Rental accommodation will experience short-term stress and vacancy rates will plummet. A consequence of this will be house price increases – potential landlords, witnessing the plunge in vacancy rates may see this as a sign of an impending house price boom and buy in to the market, creating pressure on prices. The population is boosted by the new workers, often bringing their families, and the economy enjoys a burst of activity.

Extrinsic growth drivers are the economic influences which contribute to the growth of an area, but which originate outside of that area.

To the untrained eye, the features of a strong and growing micro economy will be evident, and the temptation to get in quickly and on the ground floor creates a pseudo demand that can look like a true economic boom.

The trouble comes, of course, as soon as the project is completed. The workers move on to the next project, probably in another town, and the vacancies begin to rise. The funds which were being injected into the economy also dry up and many small businesses, which may have started or flourished during the building of the project, close down. Pressure is removed from house prices, and in fact prices drop, as distressed landlords sell up. Often, values even return to 'pre-boom' days, and investors are left with property that is difficult to rent and hard to sell.

Similar results can come from other external sources. Pure investor sentiment, where the rumour is circulating that an area is heating up and investors from all over the country vie for a small pool of available properties, can create a short-term property demand which places a false reading on true house price growth. Equally, property developers who buy up cheap parcels of land, subdivide and then engage clever marketing companies to sell the properties (often to out-of-state buyers) can also create an impression of potential growth which is never backed up by true economic vibrancy.

Intrinsic growth drivers

Intrinsic growth drivers are those factors which affect growth, but are sustainable and consistent. These are the economic influences created by a complete set of circumstances, rather than single, individual events. They are influences which can be repeated and sustained over time, and which are a sign of underlying economic growth.

Intrinsic growth drivers are those factors which affect growth, but are sustainable and consistent.

The important thing to note about intrinsic growth drivers is that some of them may look like extrinsic drivers. The difference is that more than one of them will occur at the same time, and it is the group of factors, occurring together, that separate intrinsic and extrinsic drivers more than it is the single factors alone.

Intrinsic growth drivers include:

~ *Population growth:* where the number of people who are buying property in a town is increasing at a faster rate than the national average. Property *buyers* are permanent, *renters* can be itinerant.

~ *Demographic mix:* where the types of people who live in a town are becoming more diverse. A growing area needs young people, families *and* retired people to create a community; Generally speaking, it is *community* which provides stability. Areas with a concentration in one demographic category typically grow less well than those which are more diversified.

~ *Accessibility to the area:* where transport infrastructure is consistently being upgraded and improved to allow people to move freely within, around, and out of an area.

~ *Proximity to a large centre or city:* where an area is smaller, it can still be economically vibrant when a larger area exists close by.

~ *Council's future plans for development:* where the local council is on top of the needs of its community and consistently providing for the services required at every demographic level.

As you can see, some of these intrinsic growth drivers can occur as a result of outside influences. It is the consistent and sustainable drivers which make an area a true potential hotspot in the making.

It's the depth that counts!

From this you can see that it's an important feature of property investing to understand that property investing is not just about looking for 'growth' any more than it is just about looking for cash flow.

It *is* about the depth with which you can gather the important economic data to be able to assess the true potential of an area. Doing so will provide you with a safety net of sorts, and allow you to stay in the market over the long term by considering all of the financial implications a purchase will bring.

You don't need hundreds of properties to ensure a solid financial future. You don't even need dozens of them. Eight to ten well researched and chosen areas, with sustainable growth and short-term yields high enough to manage interest rate rises and vacancies, will result in a solid, growing base of assets which will give you more choices in retirement than you ever imagined.

KEY POINTS

- ~ Growth drivers are those factors which help you to determine if an area is a *future* hotspot.
- ~ Extrinsic growth drivers result in short term, unsustainable growth.
- ~ Intrinsic growth drivers are lasting drivers which occur year in and year out and result in a stable, growing area.
- ~ In-depth study into what is driving growth is an important part of the process.

7

RISK

Nothing makes my blood boil faster than when I see an advertisement which refers to property as being a 'risk-free investment'. Such an advertisement may be referring to a rent guarantee offered for a specific property, or to a property itself built in an area experiencing current high demand. It may just be one which has had its advertisement designed by an enthusiastic real estate agent who has no qualifications in financial advising!

To suggest that any investment carries 'no risk' is highly irresponsible. All investment carries risk. While property certainly doesn't suddenly become worth nothing overnight, a poor choice can result in severe financial hardship for the buyer. This can be magnified when the buyer comes from a low financial base to begin with, as often happens when property is sold by unqualified advisers who fail to ensure the financial stability of their clients.

> To suggest that any investment carries 'no risk' is highly irresponsible.

I don't feel comfortable ever discussing an investment unless I point out the considerable risks which come with all investing. Once you are aware of the risks, and the extent to which they may affect you, then you can move ahead with an investment – or not – fully armed with all of the information you need. Until then, you are unprotected, and taking someone else's word for the risk, or safety, of any investment is simply not good enough.

Different assets

When the discussion about risk is first raised, it is usually in conjunction with a discussion about whether shares, or property, have the greatest risk. The difficulties when you try to compare the risk rating of the two are many and varied.

Firstly, a single property or share might work out exceptionally well for one investor and be the worst action another investor has ever taken, depending upon the investor's personal financial circumstances, (e.g. time till retirement and financial goals). Secondly, one share or property can be sound, or a disaster, in relation to another, depending on which one you are looking at,

...the debate should be about which investment fits most appropriately with your own needs, and your own risk profile.

and when you are looking at it. Lastly, the skill of the investor in choosing the right asset, and the right time to acquire it, also feature pretty heavily when establishing whether that asset will perform or not, and whether it carries risk to the investor, or not.

The debate about investing in any asset is not about which is best, or which carries the greatest risk. Instead, it is about which investment fits most appropriately with your own needs and your own risk profile.

Your risk profile

If you were to make an appointment with a financial planner to consult with them about investing, the very first task they would undertake would be to complete a personal risk profile.

A risk profile comes in the form of a questionnaire that you will complete. It usually contains multiple choice questions, where you are required to identify your own responses to certain financial events. It may also contain short-answer questions where you must determine what your financial goals are. This questionnaire is designed to assist the planner in guiding you toward investments which are not only appropriate to your attitude to risk, but which suit other important characteristics, such as the time you have available till you retire and your current assets and liabilities.

This is certainly a most appropriate approach to investing your money. By knowing these things, a planner can help you to choose appropriate investments which you will not spend countless hours worrying about, since they will be in keeping with your appetite for risk and your investment time horizon.

Interestingly, when many people make the decision to buy property as an investment, no such risk profile is ever completed. Considering the size of the potential investment, running to hundreds of thousands of dollars, this really seems ludicrous! It's no wonder that investors end up with property which doesn't fulfil their expectations and which they do not feel comfortable holding. In addition to this, a failed first investment will surely turn the investor off investing again and severely impact on their capacity to make sound plans for their own retirement.

I have been assisting property investors for many years, and in all that time I have found that property rarely fails people – but people fail property every time. Poor choices are usually always made because firstly, the right kind of research is not done and secondly, the risk factor attached to the property does not match that of the investor.

> Property rarely fails people – but people fail property every time.

When we talk about risk in any type of investing, three main types of risk are normally discussed:

~ General risk

~ Sector risk

~ Specific risk.

While these are generic, they very clearly relate to property just as much as they do to any other kind of investing. As such, if you are planning to start, or continue, a property portfolio, you should be aware of just how these risks relate to property and then to you.

General risk

General risk refers to the risk that you take when you make any investment, regardless of the asset type. For most people, referring to general risk equates to the potential of an investment to result in the loss of everything they own.

In any investment the chances of losing everything you *own* is rare. In some investments, the chances of losing everything you *have invested* is a possibility. With property, the chances of losing everything you *have invested* is rarer, although it is possible to lose all that you have personally contributed – perhaps your deposit or the equity portion of your own home that you placed into the investment. In some cases, and depending upon the type of property which was purchased, an investor can lose all that they have invested in that property, and more, if the property subsequently sold for less than was paid for it.

Put into perspective, severe financial loss is less likely, unless you have really been taken advantage of by someone who has fed you a host of complete lies.

In the investing world there exists a documented list of identified fears which relate to risk. While it is unclear who first coined the phrases which refer to these fears, it is now universally accepted that these categories cover the fears that most people have when investing in any asset class. They are:

1. Risk of bankruptcy.

2. Risk of returns falling short of expectations.

3. Risk of not investing in the best asset class.

4. Timing risk.

Each of these general risk categories is considered below.

Risk of bankruptcy

While, indeed, people do lose their money in all sorts of investments, the chances of losing everything when you invest in a property is usually quite limited. There could, however, be a loss of the original value of your money and, in rare cases, the loss of all that you invested. It is considered rare to end up owing more than you originally invested, although in the case of property this could eventuate where the property was a truly bad choice.

It is more likely that a bad choice of property will result in you either being returned to your original position, or finding yourself without an investment property and with a larger debt on your own home than you had when you started.

Here's an example.

Nick lived in an owner-occupied property valued at $350,000 on which he owed $150,000. His currently unencumbered equity (the part of his home which is not mortgaged, or rather the difference between what is owned and what is owed), was $200,000.

Using this equity, Nick bought another property for $250,000. He was able to borrow 80% of the purchase price of that property using the new property as security ($200,000) and for the remainder, the $50,000 plus $10,000 in purchase costs, he was able to use the unencumbered equity from his own home.

Nick now has total property worth $600,000, and total debt of $410,000. His equity is temporarily reduced to $190,000, as he had those initial costs to pay.

Nick's property doesn't go as he would have liked and he decides to sell up before it gets worse. As the entire area has not fared as well as hoped, the property Nick purchased is now only worth $225,000 and after the sale Nick nets just $220,000.

Nick's debt on that property however is $260,000, meaning he has a residual debt of $40,000. This is added to the debt he had when he began, making his new debt at this stage $190,000. The extra cost to repay this larger debt at 7% is $2,800 per annum, or around $54 a week.

This is less than ideal, but it doesn't represent a complete loss or leave Nick filing for bankruptcy. Even if Nick cannot afford the extra $54 a week and has to subsequently sell his own home, he would end up with $160,000 in cash after he repaid his debt, and so has not 'lost everything'.

In order to prevent a forced sale of his own home, Nick should, before investing, calculate his capacity to make ends meet in the unlikely event that such an outcome eventuates, and then establish if a risk to this extent is within his means.

All investors have a different capacity to withstand loss. This capacity is based on the amount of money they have to lose, the capacity they have to earn money to replace any loss and the time they have left available to earn – that is, the time available till they retire.

Before buying property, work out what the worst case scenario would cost you. How much in extra loan repayments could you afford without having to sell your own home? It is likely you have a reasonable capacity to fund an extended loan if you had to. This then becomes the true extent of this risk – a far cry from losing everything you own.

Risk of returns falling short of expectations

With any investment, and most certainly where property is concerned, the returns may be enthusiastically quoted by a salesperson or real estate agent, or they could be based on present market conditions rather than the examination of likely future market conditions. Sometimes people invest based on past performance and this can be a trap, especially when the economic landscape is not taken into account.

From a property perspective, the risk of returns varying from expectations equates to the extent to which rents differ from that which are quoted, and the degree to which you can bear that difference.

Before you buy, you can ascertain what your net cash flow position will be after settlement of the new property by using some basic cash flow calculators which take into account potential depreciation and the expected rent return. Using such calculators to vary rent return, and then assessing how much of any resulting shortfall you can afford to fund if this happens, is vital before you buy any property. By owning this book you qualify to visit my website www.destiny.com.au to download such a calculator for free.

Risk of not investing in the best asset class

The GFC brought devastation to many retirees, property owners and indeed to entire countries! It's not the first time that we have seen economic catastrophes affect otherwise relatively safe investments, and it will not be the last.

When you invest in any asset class you cannot be guaranteed its return. It was always thought that government bonds were iron clad, but since the GFC, government bonds in some countries are now at risk.

Likewise a property purchase is not a guarantee of success, although you can be fairly sure that it will always have some value. If you can afford to hold property through any downturn, history tells us that it usually bounces back within a reasonable time frame. The risk of investing anywhere must be compared against the risk of choosing something else, and then measured against your own personal risk profile.

Timing risk

At the start of this book, I bravely stated that I believe market timing is the key to getting the best return, in terms of cash flow and growth, from a property investment. I'll always stick by this, even while I agree that the longer you stay in the market, the better you are able to ride the ups and downs and see an eventual return. Market timing will always affect how great that return is, even when you have sufficient time in a market.

Knowing when to invest, and dis-invest, is also a matter of market timing, as this example shows:

Trent and Gwen both work for an energy company. Trent is 48, with 12 years till he retires, and Gwen is 57, retiring in three years.

Trent has $100,000 to invest, and buys shares in the Acme Computer Company. He buys 200,000 shares at 50 cents per share.

After six months the shares are worth $1 a share, and Trent's original investment has doubled. Wanting a share of this action, Gwen takes the $100,000 which she has been saving for retirement and invests in the same company.

Another six months pass and the Acme Computer Company shares are now worth $1.50. Gwen is ecstatic as she has increased her investment by 50%!

But two months away from her final day of work the GFC hits and the shares plummet to just 50 cents a share. Gwen has now wiped 50% off her original investment and is in trouble. Trent, however, not only retains his original investment, but still has nine years left to ride this correction through.

Applying this concept to property investing, the time in which you have to invest becomes crucial when you make the choice of what to buy and where to buy it. You must know as much as you can about the future and match expected outcomes to your own timeframes. Those with shorter timeframes will need to seek property in areas with a sound economic backdrop and immediate intrinsic growth drivers, which are impacting on values quickly. Those with longer terms till they are to retire can wait longer for growth, but may need more cash flow today, since they are more likely still raising children and meeting personal mortgage costs.

Timing for any investment is the key and the amount of risk you take should directly correlate with the amount of time you have available to ride the highs and lows.

Sector risk

Sector risk refers to the safety of one asset class as it compares to another asset class. It does not consider returns, which can weight the viability of an asset – it looks purely at the risk.

> The amount of risk you take should directly correlate with the amount of time you have available to ride the highs and lows.

When considering a specific share, there are two things which impact on its price. The first thing is the company itself, the performance of which gives a share an intrinsic value. The second is the health of the sharemarket, which gives a share its market value. In a stable market, the intrinsic value will buoy the market value, but where a sharemarket is crashing, even a share with a strong intrinsic value is likely to suffer price drops. Therefore, the risk in this sector is twofold.

Sector risk can be a difficult one to measure with property. This is because within the asset class of 'property', there are different types of property and each has its own risk level. In addition to this, as I have now clearly demonstrated, property from one area can behave differently from that in other areas, as does property in different price ranges. Unlike the sharemarket where one sector behaves consistently across all of the assets it comprises, we have many property markets which are performing differently from each other, all of the time.

So far I have considered a range of economic factors which affect the price and performance of property in individual areas. These factors can then be considered the risk factors behind how an area, and its property, will perform. This is another reason why it is so important for you to be aware of their existence and just how they affect property.

And so when it comes to sector risk, property, in relation to its risk when measured against other asset classes, would be considered to be in the low to medium range.

Cash has the lowest risk, since investing in cash, such as money in the bank, provides an immediate return. It is instantly liquid, with your original investment almost 100% guaranteed. The nature of this liquidity and guarantee is what ensures that the actual returns are low.

Fixed-interest securities, such as government and corporate bonds and term deposits, will provide a similar level of security, with slightly less liquidity. It is the restriction on access to the funds which improves the return, although this return will still be limited due to the solid guarantee you can get for the original sum you invest.

Shares rate as the highest risk because, as previously mentioned, the market can swiftly fall and big losses can result, despite any strong performance by the company in which you have invested. The liquidity is the culprit in both increasing your returns, and the risk you are exposed to by investing in shares.

Property has a high level of illiquidity, which helps to underpin its value in some way. People can't sell on a whim and the slow machine which applies to a property sale means that it is often the last thing that people sell when in trouble. As a result, when economic uncertainty occurs, properties don't flood the market as instantly as shares do. In addition to this, the fact that around 75% of all property is owner-occupied means that it is often the last asset which is liquidated by those in financial trouble. And so, the very illiquid nature of property adds to its risk level too, since it cannot be easily converted to cash to assist a financially distressed investor.

Do remember though, that property can lose value, and buying in an over-heated market may result in you holding a property worth less than you paid for it. Paying too much in the first place, by not checking your facts or buying from a club or adviser who adds commissions to the purchase price, can also result in owning a property worth less than you paid, as can buying off-the-plan and paying an assumed future price which cannot be accurately forecast.

As shown so far in this book, some of the more common risks of buying property can be easy to mitigate – ensure you buy in a proven market, with existing demand and a rising population and it's highly unlikely that you will lose money.

Specific risk

Specific risk relates to that risk which is attached to different types of property. Again, when the experts measure property risk, they are usually applying one outcome to properties from many different markets, and property of many different types, all subject to different market forces. This is why the summation about its true level of risk can be wildly wrong.

To alleviate such a risk and ensure you do not buy a property which is outside of your personal comfort zone, the next thing you must do after you have selected the right area is work out what *type* of property you should be buying. This involves two things. Firstly, it involves establishing the kind of property most in demand by the demographics of that area and then ensuring that type of property fits your risk profile.

Not all property types carry the same degree of risk. Once you know that property is an asset

...work out what type of property you should be buying.

class which suits you, it is just as important to know which type of property will most match your ultimate attitude to risk. This will then become a guide for you as to the type of property you should choose.

Here is an example of how this could go wrong.

Serge is 55 years of age, risk averse and has a small asset base. He worries that he will lose his money and so preservation of his capital is the most important thing for him.

His adviser convinces him to buy a tourism property in a hotel, because the returns are quoted as being high. For Serge this does two things: firstly he experiences high levels of stress as he sits by and watches the property suffer periods of vacancy during the off season, and secondly the property experiences short-term valuation loss until the hotel itself becomes a profit-making venture. The time for Serge to exit the strategy may end up arriving long before the property has had a chance to perform, making this a high-risk venture for Serge.

Someone who embraces risk, however, and with a long period of time until they need to see a profit, would not worry as much about short-term vacancies and will have the time available to wait for the venture to get on its feet. In addition, if the venture did in some way fail, or not turn out as well as hoped, such a person would have the time to try again with something else, and may not be as impacted by the loss as Serge would have been.

Matching property type to your own personal risk profile must be a part of your strategy.

And so you can see that knowing the level of risk each property type carries is crucial before making your choice. Matching property type to your own personal risk profile must be a part of your strategy. In many of my books, I have provided a comprehensive analysis of different kinds of property and their risk ratings. Here is a summary of that analysis.

Residential property

This includes houses and units in residential areas. While the area can have any population, you can significantly decrease your risk by choosing areas with populations of more than 15,000 people.

Such property will have a low risk compared to other property and low to medium risk compared to other investments. You can further reduce the risk by ensuring that the vacancy rates are low and on a downward trend, as this will ensure a greater likelihood of obtaining a tenant.

Holiday apartments

This category includes homes let out during holiday periods and serviced apartments which are of standard residential size. They may be managed either by a local property manager or perhaps an onsite caretaker.

These properties have a medium risk when compared to other property, because if the holiday market fails they can be converted to standard residential property. If the amount paid for one of these properties was higher than what would be paid for a similar size and style residential property, then the risk is increased. Holiday apartments are medium risk compared to other investment vehicles.

Commercial property

This includes factories, shops, warehouses and offices.

These properties have a high risk when compared to other property and a medium to high risk when compared to other investment vehicles. The risk is very high if you also borrow to buy one of these types of properties. This is because vacancies can last years and even a secure tenant can have a change of fortune and break their lease.

Niche market property

This includes hotel rooms or small hotel apartments, seniors' accommodation and student accommodation.

These properties have a high risk when compared to other property and a high risk compared to other investments. This is because they cater for a specific market and usually have no second end use – if the market it is built for fails to perform, they can be used for no other purpose. You can reduce this risk slightly by ensuring that the property you buy can easily be converted to standard residential property and that you don't pay over the market rate for it. Oversupply is a common issue with this kind of property.

Here's the catch

I am asked often what type of property is the best type to buy, with many people making the comment that, since commercial property has greater returns, it would surely make the best investment. When asked this question, I am quick to point out the relationship between different property types and your personal attitude to risk and the importance of matching a property type to your own needs for safety.

In addition to this, a risk exists if you buy a property type which is not in demand by the people who live in the area. Since demand for property, both from a renter's and a buyer's point of view, is one of the driving factors behind its capacity to grow, then you should clearly be buying the property type which will be most in demand. In an area with families, a two-bedroom unit may not be the best choice, while in a city with a significant proportion of childless couples, large family homes with big yards may not be the property most in demand.

Risk when investing, however, is not the same as other risk.

And so, once you know which property type matches your own needs for safety, you must next ensure that such a property is also in demand. If not, you may well need to find another area, one in which your preferred property type is more likely to also be the property of choice for that area's residents.

Your own risk

You might think you are pretty familiar with your own attitude to risk. Risk when investing, however, is not the same as other risk. You may enthusiastically launch yourself into a bungy jump, but feel positively nauseous at the thought of losing $50,000!

Before deciding on any type of investment, you must complete a risk profile. This applies even if you are buying property. There is a specially designed property risk profile questionnaire at the back of this book. Your risk profile will place you into one of the following risk categories:

~ *Conservative:* these investors have a low tolerance for risk and a need to preserve their capital at all costs.
~ *Stable:* this investor will have a low to medium risk tolerance level and be prepared to take very small capital risks in exchange for income.
~ *Balanced:* such an investor can stand a medium degree of risk and will do so to see both growth and cash flow.
~ *Assertive:* these investors usually have a long time until they will need to see a return and can risk their capital to get a higher than average return. They will embrace risk.

Once you know what kind of risk profile you personally have, you will be able to better choose the kind of property which most suits you, and you will also be able to choose the right kind of area, and level of gearing (more about gearing and area risk next).

This means that you can take responsibility for defraying some of the risk yourself, by overlaying your risk profile to property types and areas and choosing only those which suit you. It can be most tempting to simply buy what seems to have the best chance of a great return, but if that is outside of your capacity for risk, you may want to temper your choice a little.

Knowing your appetite for risk can also help you to avoid the temptation to make it easy for yourself by placing too much faith in the guidance of people who are trying to sell property to you. Their concerns lie purely with themselves, despite what they may tell you. Become educated about investing, know your risk profile and stick to buying properties which cater for it. From there, you will experience success, as long as you allow time to do its work.

Other property related risks

When it comes to buying property as an investment, I have identified two other areas which should be considered when you are assessing your appetite for risk. Here they are.

Gearing risk

Most people will borrow in order to buy an investment property. For a very few, the deposit for the property will be in the form of cash, while others will be using home equity.

When you use home equity it's exactly the same as using cash. If you otherwise sold your home and kept the proceeds, any equity you had would become cash in your hand. When you instead use it as security to raise a deposit on an investment property (i.e. make up the shortfall in the loan which is advanced against the new property, usually a maximum of 80% of its value), it should be considered that you are, in fact, using cash.

When you add to a cash deposit, or equity, by borrowing more to invest in property, you are multiplying the potential return on this cash. Equally, you are multiplying the potential loss too. This example explains how this works:

Judith had equity in her home of $100,000. As a lender will allow us to borrow up to 80% of our equity without lender's mortgage insurance (LMI), this essentially provides a cash sum of $80,000 to Judith, to be used as a deposit on an investment property.

Judith borrows a further $300,000 and uses it, with her 'deposit' of $80,000, to purchase a property for $365,000 (which takes her to the maximum 80% LVR). The remaining $15,000 pays her costs.

After five years this property is valued at $511,000, having grown by 7% per annum. The gross return (not considering any positive cash flow along the way) on the $380,000 invested by Judith is around 34%.

In reality, though, Judith only invested $80,000, as the rest came from her lender. If we were to consider that the cost of the lender's portion, which was $300,000, is more than likely covered by the cash in-flows, then Judith achieved a $131,000 return on her original $80,000, which is 163%. Judith's capacity to borrow has multiplied the returns on her investment.

This, of course, works in reverse too, as this example shows:

Terry had a similar capacity to unlock his equity and purchased a property for the same value as had Judith. He had seen a terrific hotel room which he purchased on the Gold Coast for $365,000, which also promised great returns. His purchase costs increased his total buy price to $380,000.

After five years it became clear that this had been a mistake, as the property suffered low occupancy and its value stumbled and then fell dramatically with the onset of the GFC. When he decided the time had come to sell, the best price he could get for his hotel room investment was $300,000.

The gross loss, not considering any positive (or in this case, negative) cash flow along the way, was 21%. However, for Terry the actual loss, considering his investment of $80,000, was 100%. The gearing for Terry had multiplied his loss.

These examples show that, the higher the gearing, the greater the risk of loss, and also the greater the capacity for return. If Judith had only borrowed 50% of her purchase price instead of 80%, then her gross return would have been only 70% instead of 163%. If Terry had borrowed only 50% of his purchase price, his loss would have been only 42% instead of 100%.

If you are using home equity to invest, you need to decide how much of it you are prepared to risk. Your own risk profile should guide you. Conservative investors should keep their gearing below the 50% LVR mark, stable investors may consider 50% to 65%, balanced investors should stay between 65% and 80% while assertive investors may be comfortable with gearing ratios of more than 80%. If you start within your own risk profile, your confidence will grow as you experience success, and you may even find that your own profile changes over time.

> The higher the gearing, the greater the risk of loss.

Elemental risk

At times I feel like I am making things up on the fly, but in truth what actually happens when I write a book is that I finally articulate what I have actually been doing on a more subconscious level for a long time!

It was only as I re-read what I had written so far, and spoke with my husband Reuben, who has been furiously working on an amazing online property tracking tool, www.destinylive.com.au, especially designed for property investors, that we began to formulate the concept of 'elemental risk'.

In many ways, elemental risk factors are those factors which you are carefully researching and considering so that you can add an extra level of protection to your investing. While I frequently speak of ensuring that you maximise your investing by always buying the best available property, in the area showing the most potential,

> Elemental risk factors are those factors which you are carefully researching and considering.

at that moment in time, I also want to encourage you to temper that advice with a consideration of your own risk profile in relation to the elements of that area.

Once you have discovered the best possible area to buy in at the time you are looking, you can use the concept of elemental risk to establish if it is also an area which you should personally be considering. If it is, then your risk profile will further serve to assist you in selecting the right property type.

Elemental risk comprises the following elements.

Area characteristics

The size of an area impacts on its capacity to grow, but also on its relative safety as an investment. Large cities with populations greater than 100,000 people present the safest choice, but may already have experienced the greatest period of property growth as its population grew. Additional infrastructure plans, new industry and other contributing factors may provide a second burst, but generally the lower risk is paid for by lower potential growth. Such an area may suit a conservative investor.

Small towns with a population lower than 15,000 would sit high on the risk scale, but with the right economic conditions may present significantly greater opportunities for growth. Assertive investors with long timeframes available would be able to invest in these areas.

Sitting in between, I'd suggest that areas with a population between 15,000 and 50,000 would suit a balanced investor, as such an area, where the right conditions exist, would be ramping up as a great investment, but may have already started a growth spurt. Those towns where the population is between 50,000 and 100,000 may fit into the risk profile of a stable investor, as the growth has already been proven, but is not yet over.

Note that areas can also change in terms of risk as they grow.

Many years ago, just before I began to invest in property, I heard of an investor who was buying property in Elizabeth in South Australia. That entire region had a population of around 30,000 and he was buying duplex units for around $25,000 each. He was a young guy and so he had plenty of time up his sleeve, and if this turned out to be a bad investment, plenty of opportunity to recover any lost capital. Since I had always considered myself a stable investor, it was not until around five years ago, when the population sat at 60,000, that I started to become interested in Elizabeth. By that time, the prices for those same duplex units had reached almost $100,000, and I kicked myself for not buying at $25,000! Still, I could see more to come and so I invested in five duplex units.

Today as the population heads toward 100,000 opportunities still exist but the area has become more one for a conservative investor. Due to its bright future, there is little risk involved in buying there, but the capacity for values to again quadruple is now well and truly gone. It's still a great area to buy, but assertive investors may not find appeal there any longer.

The size of the area is not a direct precursor to good returns. There are just as many areas with smaller populations which have not grown, and likely never will. Just like everything I have written about in this book, population size must be considered in concert with other factors to determine if the direction of that area is moving forward.

Other elemental factors

Just as the size of the population places an area in a specific risk category, so do other characteristics about that area. These characteristics can be considered together to help you paint a picture about the elements which need to exist in an area and property to ensure it best matches your risk profile. Again, this is by no means an exact science and it should only be considered as a further layer to help you obtain the most appropriate investment for you.

I have prepared a table to assist you to quickly see the elements each level of investor will most require. The reason I have included this table here is to give you a further guideline which will make choosing the right property, and area, easier for you. Further, for those people who are really into

Profile	Vacancy Rate	Purchase Price	Property Type	Title Arrangements	Rental Type	Portfolio LVR	Property Cash Flow
Conservative	<0.5%	<$250,000	Residential house or unit	Torrens or Strata	Permanent >12 months	<50%	>$20 pw
Stable	<1.5%	<$300,000	Residential house or unit	Torrens or Strata	Permanent >6 months	<50% to 65%	<$20 pw to <$20 (L) pw
Balanced	<3%	<$350,000	Residential house or unit, small commercial or student	Torrens or Strata, company	Permanent >6 months, month to month, holiday let	<65% to 80%	$20 (L) to <$50 (L) pw
Assertive	<5%	<$500,000	All property types	All arrangements	All rental types	<80%	>$50 (L) pw

Note: (L) refers to the loss, or negative cash flow an investor is likely to be able to withstand each week.

do-it-yourself options, www.mypropertymatch.com.au will be released in 2011. This new online system will be a great asset for investors, so watch out for that! In the meantime, here is a quick summary table showing how these characteristics relate to the different risk profiles.

Remember, this is purely a guide, an extra level against which you can measure your appetite for risk. As with all guides, this is by no means absolute and you should always talk to a Qualified Property Investment Adviser (QPIA®) about any property investment you might like to make.

KEY POINTS

~ Shares and property cannot really be compared in terms of risk since they are such different assets.

~ You must consider your personal risk profile in regard to investing in property as an asset class and the type of property you ultimately buy.

~ General risk applies to the risk of investing in any asset. It considers the chances of losing your money or getting a lower return than hoped.

~ Sector risk refers to the risk of buying property when compared to the risk of buying something else.

~ Specific risk refers to the risk of buying one property type over another.

~ Gearing risk refers to the multiplication of risk which occurs when you borrow to invest.

~ Elemental risk looks at the area you are buying in, and its elements, such as population size.

~ All property investors should complete a personal risk profile before starting a portfolio.

FINDING THE PROPERTY

8

Where to start? It's all a little like the chicken and the egg. I've told you how to uncover areas which display the economics required for them to become hotspots. The problem is, you can only find out this information once you have picked an area to start looking into. You could spend days or even months exploring an area, only to find at the end that it isn't suitable and you have to start again somewhere else!

Buying in hotspots is actually easy – others are probably already doing it and you're likely to be hearing about these areas consistently in the press. Buying in warm spots is much harder, though not impossible, and takes a lot more of your time. But the rewards are many and include the chance to buy at extremely low prices and get not only an instant boost in values, once other investors also discover it, but the likelihood of increasing yields too, since the factors which drive values growth are also often those which drive demand for rentals.

To buy in a warm spot, you need to almost start with the

dartboard approach – throw a dart at the map, and then research all of the areas which surround its point of impact. An examination of those broad economic characteristics should help you to decide quite quickly if that area is worth further research, and will often result in you simply pulling out the dart altogether and having another throw. This is where the time factor comes in – this type of work can take countless hours. But, if along the way you uncover an area which stacks up after due diligence, and which no-one else yet knows about, the time expended may well be very worth your while.

The point about finding warm spots and then having an element of faith to invest in them is this – as long as you have followed my suggestions for due diligence and consulted my book, *The 20 Must Ask Questions® for Every Property Investor* (published by Wiley) the area will be at least stable and you're unlikely to buy a complete lemon. The flipside of that coin is, of course, the very real chance that buying property this way may mean that you really do get in on the ground floor of the next great hotspot. I guess the real skill lies in knowing where to start, and how to actually put the theory of finding the next hotspot into a practical process which can be followed.

> The real skill lies in knowing where to start.

Of course there is no magic formula to help you to find the next hotspot, nor is there a quick and easy shortcut. Many people I meet tell me they lack the time required to do this for themselves and they need to find someone who can do it for them. You have to realise early on that if someone is going to do this job for you, they are likely doing it for others too, and you are right back to only getting second-hand news when it may be too late to get the big gains you are chasing. If the job of putting together your retirement portfolio and working towards a sound financial future is important enough for you, then you might have to give up something now to get there. For me, it means allocating time late at night, and potentially losing sleep, to put in the long hours I know are necessary to get this right. For you, it may mean giving up something else, but if time is your issue then there is no doubt something will have to go for you.

As you attack the task more often you will begin to develop a kind of sixth sense which will serve to reduce the time spent on the process for future purchases. By instinct you will begin to be able to spot a warm spot at ten paces, and not waste your time on areas which will never stack up.

I've referred often in this book to the fact that the best property at the moment in time you are looking is unlikely to be near where you live now. You may be uncomfortable buying away from where you live or sight unseen, but not doing so will severely limit your choices and your chances of ultimate success. If you are going to tackle this job of picking hotspots with any seriousness, you must first deal with the issue of not needing to buy near where you live.

Where to buy

It's highly unlikely that the next hotspot is going to be anywhere near your house, nor will it even be in your state! You need to be fully prepared for the fact that the area you find to invest in will be a long way from where you live, and unless you have dealt with the issues some people have about buying sight unseen, you are going to find it hard to take the plunge and make the investment.

Here are some things you need to know.

~ While you think you 'know' the area you live in, in reality what you know about your area relates to lifestyle, not investment. Remember that features such as accessibility to a bus stop, school and shopping centre, and the general attractiveness of an area, only become important once you get to the property selection phase of the process. This phase is one of the last things that you do. Allowing these types of physical, lifestyle features to guide you in your choice may mean that you overlook those greater economic characteristics which are far more important. In addition, often the lifestyle features of an area are developed after you buy there. While the area is 'pre-hotspot', many of the things that add to sustainability of an area are yet to be provided. This is why it is a potential hotspot, rather than a hotspot.

~ With thorough due diligence and reference to my 20 Questions®, you can know the area you eventually invest in even better than you know the one you live in now. When you consider the detailed information which these questions uncover, you can see how knowledgeable you can become in a relatively short space of time. More importantly, that knowledge will be the kind from which you can make valid purchase decisions without emotion.

~ Looking at a property doesn't change its outcome as an investment – the qualities which make a good investment are not physical. In fact looking at it can often cause you to overlook the more important features, because a physical inspection generally leads to an emotional attachment of some kind.

Alternatively, looking at a property may lead to a rejection of a property which would otherwise make a great investment, purely on the basis that you were turned off by its lack of physical appeal. For those of you who are thinking that not viewing a property may result in a purchase of a property with serious and expensive structural defects, I pose the question: "Would you actually be able to recognise such defects if you inspected the property?" Probably not, and this is why we employ qualified building inspectors after we have made the decision to buy.

~ You may feel you have an instinct for what people like as a place to live, but you don't. You cannot think or feel like the person who is going to be your tenant, so only buying what you would personally live in is not a valid selection criterion.

~ The area doesn't need to be currently popular or in a special location. In fact, the words 'location location' haven't really applied that well to property investing, with many areas situated in what you might think of as a bad location eventually performing incredibly well from a growth point of view. Your personal feelings need to be put aside.

~ People often buy near where they live because they want to be able to 'look after' the property themselves. This can do little more than add unnecessary stress to the process for you, and as I have mentioned earlier, you most likely lack the skills to do a good job of property management anyway. As you build your portfolio, you will not have time to look after these properties.

Once you have accepted all of those points, you will be more mentally ready to begin your dartboard approach to starting or continuing your investment portfolio.

Sourcing the areas and the properties

In our increasingly digital times, your first research tool will probably be the internet, particularly as it allows you to search nationally without leaving your desk. This will ensure that you don't miss interstate opportunities that we have established will very likely offer superior property to that in your own suburb or neighbourhood. To add depth to your research there are plenty of people who are willing to 'help'. Let's now look at all of the possible resources you can use to source the right investment property now.

1. Using on-line tools

Now that the web has become a daily tool for most of us, it has also become the number one source of property for any type of buyer. Roughly 80% of the work which needs to be done on area selection, and then property selection, is done via the internet. I personally love that fact as it considerably reduces the time taken to find property. If I have to *go* somewhere to carry out any tasks in my search for property, I have to get ready – shower, hair, make-up and put on suitable clothing. There's an extra hour straight up each time there is a new task to do. Using the internet means that I can just walk down the hall to my computer and I am away.

In order to commence using those magnificent web-based resources which are at your fingertips, you need an actual starting point. Tempting as it is to simply grab a copy of the latest property investing magazine and follow the listed hotspots, I prefer to uncover my own areas as the aim, remember, is to find an area which is 'pre-hotspot'.

To start, use Google® Maps to find an area or region to focus on. I love Google® Maps because it has zoom capabilities and I can start broadly and then get closer and closer to areas, right down to street level if necessary.

Commence with a known region and then begin to drill down into the areas within that region. Avoid starting with those areas which you know are red hot, and keep away from those really big capital city CBD areas, as, by now, few of them have the significant drivers required to provide that 'burst' of growth you are looking for during your period of ownership.

When you first begin, you are trying to establish a general region in which to start fine-tuning your research. You will be asking questions relating to economic vibrancy and attempting to establish the economic landscape which you learned about in our earlier economics lesson. To do this, a search of 'regional economic data' on an area you have chosen using any search engine will return a number of results.

At this stage you are attempting to paint an economic landscape, you are not looking for actual property. It can be so tempting to also start your search for property right now, but that will only serve to turn your focus to property type and price, and you may end up finding a fantastic property, at a great price, in a lousy area.

Once you are uncovering regions with suitable economic statistics, you can begin to narrow down to 'local government areas'. The Australian Bureau of Statistics (ABS) provides free census data around these local government areas and the council websites often provide economic briefs which are developed around known statistics. These briefs can be a great way to know what the council has on its planning drawing-board, as well as whether these projects are funded, or not. Remember, unfunded projects are wishes, while funded projects are real plans that will occur.

Next, go to real estate specific websites. You are not doing this to find actual property. Rather, sites such as www.domain.com.au and www.realestate.com.au include short suburb reports and recent sales data. This data can often round out your research with additional evidence to support what the general economic data is telling you.

There are literally dozens of other companies and sites which use web-based resource centres to provide the kind of information and data which will be most useful to you. They come and go and to list them here would limit your search. Internet search engines are quite intuitive and I find that if I simply pose a question around what it is I need to know, and type it into the search box, I usually get a large number of hits, many containing pieces of information which I can use.

Lastly, local newspapers are all online these days and they can be a great added source of listings. In addition to that you can access other great and useful information from the local news. News can be slow in a smaller area, and any rumour, plan or protest is likely to make the papers. By finding the local newspapers in the area where your search is taking place you can often get quick snapshots of what is happening at ground level. Many have detailed information about council activity and they certainly quickly report any murmurings about transport and other infrastructure development.

2. Property spruikers

Property spruikers sell their wares in a variety of ways. At their free investment seminars, they may offer, as a solution to your financial woes, property for which they gain a commission. Or, they may disguise themselves as a club of some sort, offering mentoring and peer support, while taking commissions and developer kickbacks under the table without your knowledge.

You may indeed discover property which seems to suit your needs from these sources, but a word of warning: generally any kind of club, group or association which claims to be able to assist property investors to buy property will often provide very subjective views about the areas in which the properties they are selling are located. In addition to this, it is prudent to point out that they are only providing you with information about the areas in which they personally can sell a property. While that area may indeed be a good area, it may not be the *best* area available at that moment in time, nor might it be currently in the phase of cash flow or growth which exactly matches your own needs.

Be cautious of spruikers endorsing any of the numerous property investment clubs around the country. In reality these are usually little more than sales agents spruiking property above market price, with club members taking commissions. These commissions are likely to be built into the property's price and could be as much as 10%. You are not required to be told about them, since technically you are not the one paying them, but make no mistake, it is paid from somewhere, and the purchase price paid by you is likely to reflect these additional commissions, somewhere.

Some clubs claim to be 'non profit', and while I have seen

small groups of genuine individuals who form social groups and share the common interest of property investing, formal groups which advertise are never really non-profit. The use of people considered to be your 'peers' is actually a clever marketing ploy adopted by many of these clubs, which have many levels (containing people who share in commissions) and are little more than pyramid selling schemes.

If registration with such a group is free, and you feel that pressure will not be applied to you by joining, it may be suitable to complete such a registration. If you do so, make sure you research not only the group, but the property it offers. Ensure this research is independent of any material provided to you by the group. Find out what their cut is. Some commissions may be reasonable and in line with the commissions any real estate agents would be entitled to when they marketed and found buyers for a vendor's property.

The two biggest dangers with such a group is buying a property in an area which is not the best available area at that time, and buying a property which is priced more highly than similar properties, not owned by that club. I have seen a significant number of cases where properties purchased through such clubs have been sold at more than $60,000 over market value. These clubs will have seemingly legitimate valuers in their stable too, so any property suggested should have its value confirmed by your own, independent valuer.

3. Property exhibitions and home shows

Once you have already carried out your initial research, and have gathered information about areas which fit the criteria to be a potential hotspot, it may be useful to attend a property expo or home show. These expos run annually in the state capitals. They are well advertised and can be worth a visit if you attend with the objective of gaining some further education to supplement your own research. One attraction of home shows or property expos is that they run reasonably-priced (or even free) education programs in the form of seminars or workshops and often feature expert keynote speakers.

It's useful to remember the aim of the exhibitors at such an event. The costs of involvement are significant, and it is crucial that each exhibitor achieve the maximum amount of sales possible to cover these costs and make their attendance at the show worthwhile. The best way to make a sale is to obtain early emotional involvement from a potential buyer – this involvement is known to make it very difficult to say no. Even the most astute investors often find the pull of a potential investment, if presented well enough, difficult to resist.

Bear in mind that many exhibitors at such an event are selling a *product*. With the exception of the few independent advisers who may attend, they are not there to provide you with guidance as to the best area for you to buy, and it's unlikely any one of them would carefully assess your personal situation and then tell you that their product does not suit you.

To help you to become engaged in their product, they will likely have a range of physical tools – exact miniature model buildings, display rooms, glossy brochures and interactive DVDs or web-based tools which look amazing and seem to point to that product as being perfect for you.

Many exhibitors will do their best to gain a commitment from you on the spot, and some may even have contracts to sign which can be hard to get out of. Always use any information you might acquire from one of these shows to add to your list of possible areas, and don't make any decisions about any property on the day that you see it. Put some space between you and the offer, and then carry out the same amount of due diligence as you would on an area which you came upon without the benefit of marketing material.

4. Marketing agents

Where new properties are concerned, there is always an abundance of development going on all around the country. In days gone by such property was marketed locally via the newspaper and from on-site sales offices.

These days, few developers fail to overlook the considerable advantages of employing a nationwide marketing strategy implemented by a marketing agent or a marketing representative. They are aware that potential buyers exist all over Australia, and in some respects it can be easier to sell property to someone who is less familiar with an area than to a local.

There are several marketing strategies employed by these developers. Some may utilise the services of a telemarketing company that phones you to either arrange an appointment in your own home or to invite you to attend an 'investment seminar'. Rarely is the actual product mentioned in such target marketing. Rather, the focus is on painting for you a desired outcome – that is, wealth creation – which compels you to attend. The risk is cleverly reversed – instead of the risk of you not attending this seminar being placed with the developer, the risk that you may retire without wealth if you *don't* attend now sits with you.

Of course, once you are in that seminar room, or the salesperson is in your own home, the guilt trip continues to be placed upon you, until the magic solution – the property they have to offer – is presented.

The problem, of course, is that property selection should never come before area selection and when you buy property in this manner you are basing your decision essentially upon how you feel about the property itself. Before you even get to property selection, a detailed analysis of the area should have been carried out. While the developer may have suitable figures available about the area in which the property is located, this doesn't allow you to effectively analyse and compare it to other areas. You should have already chosen the area long before you even begin to look at actual property.

The other issue with buying property in this manner is that it may be overpriced, having had a range of commissions built in. While you may feel that it is acceptable to pay slightly over a market price in return for removing the time-consuming responsibility of doing the hard work yourself, remember that this *only* applies if that property happens to exist in an area which is the best available choice at that moment in time, and it also matches your immediate needs for cash flow, or growth!

5. The local real estate agent

There is no question that a telephone call to the local real estate agent is a must. While we can find property on line easily enough, the considerable benefits of forming a relationship with local real estate agents cannot be ignored. Most properties are listed on real estate websites, but not all of them are. In addition to this, if you have a good relationship with local agents, you might be lucky enough to be informed about new listings before they are actually marketed. A good agent will farm his database prior to spending any money on marketing, although, do note that I am talking about those 'good agents'.

I have to say that real estate agents can and have been the bane of my life! I have found some sensational ones, but equally I have been exposed to some dreadful examples of real estate agents too. Surprisingly, many of these same agents work in areas struggling to get sales, and one would think that this would make them follow up every lead possible.

I also have had very funny experiences with agents who seem to have little clue. Just recently, I made a formal offer, in writing, on a property which was listed as 'offers over $230,000'. My market research indicated that the market value was actually lower than that and so I offered $215,000.

I received a return email with the following comment:

"Just a note about your offer. You seem to be new at this (note to agent: *know your client!*). I find that a vendor is more likely to accept an offer from a buyer if it is closer to the asking price!"

I am sure that you find that response as hilarious as I did. After I picked myself up from the floor, I wrote back and said "Yes. And I am equally sure that your vendor's asking price is more likely to be paid if it's closer to the market value!!" Needless to say that despite the considerable evidence I provided to this agent about true market values, she failed to encourage her vendors to even counter-offer, and now, many weeks later, that property is still on the market."

Just the very next day a call came through on my mobile phone. It sounded like a 10 year old who introduced themselves simply as "John's PA". When I asked why they were calling, he or she (I couldn't tell as this person truly sounded like a young child), responded with 'It's about the property".

"What property?" I asked.

"The one in Werribee. You put in an internet enquiry".

I racked my brain until I recalled that, six months prior I *had* placed an internet enquiry about a property in that area. I am sure I couldn't hide my disbelief when I answered "Are you kidding? That was six months ago!"

"Yeah well, are you still interested?"

It was school holidays, and clearly that agent had recruited his primary school child to make all of those calls he had been too lazy to make when they were due!

They won't all be like that, though, and many will go out of their way to assist you. That said, always remember what real estate agents do for a living – they are skilled and qualified to sell you the physical aspects of any property but they cannot give you financial or investment advice. They cannot know if the property in question is right for your personal circumstances, and very few real estate agents are aware of, or even understand, property investing. So, don't have expectations they cannot fulfil, and don't ask questions which you know it is in their best interests to answer with whatever they think you want to hear.

A real estate agent will use one of several methods to market a property:

Exclusive listing

In this scenario the property will only be available through that real estate agent. They may well still list it on the internet but only that agent can introduce you to the property.

Multi-listing

Any agent may introduce you to a property, but the agent who actually lists the property will receive part of the sales commissions.

Auctions

An auction is a physical process. You must either be there, or otherwise have a body on the ground on your behalf to make the bids for you. This is slowly changing, with a few new online auction sites having recently been launched, but until this trend takes off, your presence will be required. It simply will not be prudent for you to be jetting off all around the country attending auctions that you only have a slight chance of winning, and it's unlikely that you will know people in the area you end up selecting as the next hotspot to do this for you.

Emotional issues exist here too – even if you *can* manage to attend an auction in the very place identified as suitable for investing, auctions are a hot-bed of swirling emotions which normally result in someone paying too much for a property. Part of the process you have undertaken when you completed your due diligence was to establish potential cash flow. Since an auction is unpredictable, and the competitiveness of the event can result in even the most level-headed of people making that one last bid to outbid the other buyer, the risk is that your original cash flow analysis will be blown away and you end up with a property generating an entirely different cash flow than expected. Remember that overpaying can result in a longer period of time before you obtain enough equity to leverage into another property, and that extra $10,000 at the outset could magnify into slowing down your entire property investment strategy.

Auctions have very little place in the life of a property investor.

Buyers' advocates

I am including this under the heading of real estate agents because a buyer's advocate (sometimes called buyer's agent) must be a licensed real estate agent. In recent years we have seen more and more buyers' advocates offering services to property investors. Though the original intention of a buyer's agent was to assist owner-occupiers, these days we see them competing in the property investment arena more and more.

The way it works is that a buyer will appoint an agent or advocate to source property for them, according to a brief outlining their wants/desires/needs in a property. Usually the buyer has already pinpointed an area where they want the buyer's advocate to search. Often the buyer's advocate will be appointed because they have local knowledge in this area. The cost of this service can be as much as 10% of the property's price, or more. The vendors will also usually be paying a real estate agent to market the property for them so the agent's sales commission will also be taken into account in the sale price.

You may think that securing the services of a buyer's advocate will save you a lot of time and therefore be worth the expense. But remember that you still have to choose the area yourself, and it is this part of your research that needs the most effort and care with reference to your own needs. Also consider that as you build your investment property portfolio it becomes a costly exercise to use a buyer's advocate every time you want to buy another property.

As the name suggests, these people or organisations are acting for the buyer in the buying process. They are not usually property investment advisers and the information that they can provide to you will be limited to the property itself. In essence, they are acting for you in the negotiation phase, and the major work towards choosing the right area in which to buy must still be carried out by you.

I'd suggest that, for the fee that you pay each time you engage an advocate to buy on your behalf, you might consider instead investing in a one-off, negotiation skills course, or attend a property investment education course which includes negotiation skills. Even if the cost of such a course was equal to engaging an advocate once, you will then have the skills for life to use again and again.

Putting it all together

As previously mentioned, some years ago I wrote the *Pocket Guide to Investing in Positive Cash Flow Property* (published by Wiley). Regardless of whether you are looking for areas in the values growth phase of the cycle, or those in the yield growth phase, that book will provide a step-by-step process to use to secure a property. It does not have the comprehensive information you need to get a good educational background to property investing, but once you have that, the book will ensure you don't miss any important steps.

This is where the hard work and commitment must truly begin. I have met many property investors who, each time I meet them continue to tell me that they have been actively looking for property for months, sometimes years, but have not yet found the right property. I feel this isn't possible – there are so *many* opportunities available, it's simply not feasible to suggest that months of the right kind of activity uncovers nothing.

I'd like to suggest that anyone who tells me this is actually experiencing analysis paralysis. It can take so much effort to carry out alot of this research that the detail alone becomes a barrier to moving forward. Becoming too involved in the data can actually prevent investors from making that purchase, as they continue to uncover small defects or issues which make the area seem less than perfect.

No area is going to present itself as the perfect potential hotspot – all areas will have some kind of drawback. This is where an element of faith and alot of trust must come in. If the major economic drivers appear to be present, and one or two 'kickers', such as some employment or infrastructure projects are in existence, then you have to rely on local government to eventually provide the services and infrastructure which such a growing community will require. The point is, if everything is already in place, it will be either a raging hotspot *right then*, or it's past the hotspot phase and into its 'solid' phase. Either way, it's probably too late for you.

KEY POINTS

~ It's easy to buy in hotspots but much harder to buy in 'warm spots'. Warm spots may deliver a better outcome.

~ You do *not* know the area you live in well enough to invest there and thinking you do is not a good reason to buy where you live.

~ Use many resources for buying property – the internet, real estate agents, local newspapers.

~ Be careful of property clubs, auctions and developers.

~ Invest in a good negotiation skills course.

CLARIFYING
MICRO DATA

Once you are at the stage where you have accumulated significant economic data about general regions, it is time to take this to its most basic level so that you can select an actual suburb within that area which has the best prognosis for investment potential.

Earlier, I mentioned that, initially, choosing between different suburbs in an area where strong growth drivers seem to exist should not be a consideration for you. Area selection is about an economic overlay, not about the beauty or popularity of individual suburbs.

By this stage, however, you are coming very close to actually selecting a property, and you'd like to be sure it's in a suburb likely to experience great growth in both values and rental yields.

You'll note that I have never used the expression 'buy in the best suburb'. I have countless tales to tell about properties that I, and my clients, have purchased in areas which are considered to be far from the 'best suburbs'. I've bought in suburbs with nasty nicknames, ones which make nearby residents cringe when you mention them. Terry Ryder calls them 'Ugly Duckling' suburbs, due to the propensity of many of these areas to turn into beautiful swans.

That doesn't mean that you should be selecting an area and suburb based on the fact that it is an ugly duckling. Many ugly ducklings also grow up to be hideous swans, but it's usually the ones with qualities which are obviously not going to be tempered by maturity!

I have found, interestingly enough, that one suitably vibrant area, with many suburbs all at different price-points, will experience similar growth across *all suburbs* within that area. Further, in many cases, those suburbs which are initially at the bottom of the ladder, in terms of their value and popularity, can often achieve better growth records than their more expensive counterparts.

I've considered why this is, and I believe it's because:

~ In areas where factors exist to limit urban sprawl (such as areas on a peninsula) once the area becomes popular and the 'best houses' are gone, people will want to buy *any* property just to get in. Where there is a 'bad side' of an area and a 'good side', the lines of demarcation frequently become blurred over time.

~ In areas where there is a significant difference between properties at the top of that market and those at the bottom, when those at the top become too pricey, more people seek those in the lower price brackets. More pressure is brought to bear on this lower market and pressure equals demand, which equals growth.

~ People will more often buy cheaper properties because they believe that they can fix them up for a total lower cost than buying a property where everything is already done. Again, this results in pressure on these lower priced properties which translates into greater growth.

Again I stress that you must not buy in an ugly duckling suburb just *because* it's an ugly duckling suburb! However, it's acceptable to buy property in the ugly duckling suburb of an area which shows overall economic vibrancy. I will go so far as to suggest that, at times, it may be *better* to buy in such suburbs. That fact has certainly proved correct in my own portfolio.

Exceptions to the rule of lower-priced property growing well

While they are few in number, there will be exceptions to the rule that lower priced suburbs can still grow very well.

Once again, it is hard to pinpoint the exact factors which hold an area back. I've looked at many of these areas and tried to ascertain what is really going on. To the best of my ability, here are some features which may exist in suburbs which fail to thrive.

Unemployment

A significant portion of the population is unemployed. While a high unemployment rate does not mean that an area will not do well, I have found that an area with high unemployment *and* no significant infrastructure planning or new housing development plans may fail to progress for many years. The point to note here is that where a new housing development, complete with master planning of shopping centres and schools, is on the drawing board, that area may split into two. The newer area will attract employed families with median incomes and the older area will remain as it is *for a time*. Often under these circumstances, once that newer part of town is well established, then the older area comes under demand and we see a significant shift in the demographics.

An aging population

I am not referring to an area with a population characterised by a significant portion of already retired people. Where the population is retired, and the area shows economic vibrancy, then it may well be an area which is about to become a hotspot, as the retired population move on to 'greener pastures' and younger families tend to move in. But where a population is aging, and the average age of residents is well above the national average of around 37 years, it may be an area about to enter an exceptionally stagnant phase. This is because we have a significant part of our population who are underprepared for retirement, and many of these people live in some of those lower socio economic areas. Again, somewhat like the chicken and the egg, they are probably living in those areas *and* underprepared for retirement because they are in a lower socio economic group. Such people will remain in their homes throughout their retirement and when property does not turn over its value stagnates.

Areas can, and do, change their demographic makeup.

High crime rates

An exceptionally high crime rate can often occur in tandem with high unemployment. While you can buy in an ugly duckling suburb with a high crime rate, it has to be one with significant growth drivers in place. Areas can, and do, change their demographic makeup and do become more attractive and valuable even where the crime rates today are high. But this only happens if significant effort is being expended by council and law enforcement authorities to change the situation.

We have personally purchased in many ugly duckling areas with great success. Before doing so, our substantial research into those areas ensured that we had our eyes wide open and were aware of the potential of those areas.

How many 'listings' is too many?

I've known investors to look into an area, see that there are, say, 1,200 properties on the market, and refuse to look any more because they have assessed an oversupply. Those same investors may then buy in an area where only 600 properties are on the market, feeling happier about this number.

Where is the problem, I hear you ask? The problem is that it is not the number of properties on the market which is important, it's the number in relation to the population, which holds the key.

I wish I could provide you with an actual formula – an acceptable number of available properties per capita – but I haven't really worked that one out yet. There's a bit of instinct required here, but at least I can tell you that you will know when there are *too* many. Equally important is the fact that the number of listings is also relevant to that economic data that I keep harping on about. There may be a great number of listings, but if the economic landscape looks red hot, then the good news about such a large number of listings is that you will be spoiled for choice! Under those circumstances you can be pretty sure that the situation of oversupply is going to be short-lived, especially if population forecasts are for a booming population growth.

I recently considered two areas in which to buy. One had 1,600 properties on the market and the other had 800. The former had a population of 110,000, which in essence meant that there were 1.4 properties available for every 100 people. The latter had 16,000 people, which meant there were five properties available for every 100 people. Given that the smaller area also had less economic vibrancy, it was easy to see which one to choose.

As with all of the factors you are discovering, all things must be relative and considered in concert with the other data you are collecting. Low vacancy rates are only relative to the reasons why they are low; high demand for available properties must be considered in terms of the current rate of population growth; and the actual number of properties on the market must be measured against the total number of people *and* what the area is doing, economically speaking.

From all of the actions you have so far taken, you should be able to narrow down a shortlist of areas which seem to satisfy your personal needs for either cash flow or growth, which suit your personal risk profile and are areas which have some big ticks in the pro box in terms of their economic vibrancy. You are more than likely ready to find an actual property.

Conclusion

This book may seem a little like it contains a lot of bits and pieces. In fact, while my intent in writing it was to be able to provide a sound dissertation on economic landscaping, and help all property investors to begin investing as if they live in the 21st century, I also am aware that my past books do not contain a lot of the other more recent lessons I have been providing lately through my TV shows and seminars.

Every year I present a seminar in each capital city. The purpose of that seminar is to provide new information to all property investors and to keep them up to date with the latest property investing strategies.

I always have something new to relate and at times I need to update old information to keep it relevant for today. Other times, as I am discussing something with an individual property investor, a great thought might occur to me and I furiously research and develop that thought so that it becomes another lesson.

And so, from this point in the book, I'd like to provide some of those lessons which are about specific aspects of property investing, so that they can help you to become a better property investor. These lessons may have nothing to do with the general economic overview that this book is intended to provide, but they are important things for you to know as a property investor.

KEY POINTS

~ Once you have the data, you must clarify it.

~ You don't have to buy in the 'best suburb' of an area which is becoming a hotspot – most suburbs are likely to become the best suburb.

~ Lower priced suburbs often have the greatest degree of growth.

~ There are some small exceptions to the rule of lower-priced areas growing well.

~ The number of listings available does not give clues as to whether the market is in oversupply – it's the number of listings in relation to the size of the population.

10

BOOSTING CASH FLOWS

At time of writing, the world has come through one of its greatest financial crises on record, and some say there is more to come. For now, we have landed at a place we have never really been before where, like the butterfly effect, our global markets respond instantly to murmurs being heard half a world away.

Technology is the culprit and also the reason why the outcome is so hard to determine. History is simply not repeating itself, and so we, as reluctant players in the drama, must strap ourselves in, hang on for the ride and hope that it comes to an end before we suffer any real damage.

Australia hasn't been immune to the GFC, and property investors in some markets are feeling the pinch. While-ever we have such uncertainty around the economy, we can also never be sure about interest rates.

You may be using this uncertainty as an excuse not to invest. If your personal cash flows are truly that tight, then I would agree that now may not be the time. While I'm quite confident that rates won't move too far, and while each interest rate movement can be somewhat offset by an additional tax deduction and probably even an increase in rent, I never recommend that anyone buy property if they are struggling financially.

If, on the other hand, you feel that you can manage through these unstable times, or you are an investor who currently owns property which has had a blow to its cash flow because of interest rate increases, here are some tips that may help.

Claim your deductions now

This is obvious to a lot of investors, but many people still like to wait till the end of the year to make their deductible claims so that they can get a lump sum of money back.

This makes no sense. The tax office will not pay interest to you for the privilege of holding your money for the year. You, on the other hand, can *save* interest by using the tax you can get back from your deductions to make additional repayments into your loan, offsetting interest and adding a small amount to your cash flows.

To do this, you have to obtain an Income Tax Withholding Variation (ITWV) form, from the Australian Tax Office (ATO). You can even download one of these from www.ato.gov.au. Using this form, you must estimate the income you are to receive from your property, the expenses you will have throughout the year, and also the amount of depreciation you will be able to claim on the building, fixtures, fittings and furniture. For those who have held their property for some time, this information is easy to obtain, especially if you have been

> The tax office will not pay interest to you for the privilege of holding your money for the year.

diligent with tracking your expenses and income. Those who have only just purchased will need to obtain past figures from the agent, or make as close an estimation as they can. Depreciation is easy – simply have a depreciation schedule prepared by a reputable quantity surveyor, and you will have the exact figures for each year, for the entire life of the allowable depreciation.

Once you have completed the form and lodged it, it will be assessed and your employer will be advised of how much to reduce your tax to be withheld. The amount will be based on how much you have already paid for the financial year, and so it is important that you complete a new form at the start of each financial year.

In many cases the cost to add value has no marked effect on the ability to increase rent.

If you are worried that you will over- or under-estimate, and so incur a penalty from the tax office for doing so, don't be. As long as you keep track of your income and expenses, you should be able to tell within around two months of the end of the financial year how close you have been. If you are more than 10 per cent out either way, there will still be time to lodge another form rectifying this, prior to the year coming to an end.

Receiving your tax breaks weekly in your pay could provide an extra $40 or $50 a week to you, and this could mean the difference between being able to manage the costs, or having to sell up.

Adding value

This is a method that I am not quick to recommend, as in many cases the cost to add value has no marked effect on the ability to increase rent. However, if you decide to explore this option, there are some things you must do.

Firstly, work out exactly how you intend to add value, and establish if it is an action which is likely to impact on your yield. For example, a property in a tropical climate may be more in demand and command a higher rent return if you install an air conditioner, whereas such an improvement may mean little to someone who rents property in Melbourne or Adelaide. The addition of a bedroom could be the solution if your property is in an area where people demand property with more bedrooms than you currently have, but where your property is typical of the average home and already satisfies demand nicely, it may not be worth it. Aesthetic enhancements such as gardens, new paint and carpets or an upgraded kitchen may add an appeal that brings more tenants, but may not impact greatly on how much they will pay.

Be guided by your property manager in this regard, and then do a cost benefit analysis. For example, a new kitchen may cost $10,000, which at 8.5% interest will cost an extra $850 a year in interest on your loan. You would need to achieve an extra $17 a week in rent to

You are not looking to add value to achieve a higher sales price – you are after more rent.

pay for this. Alternatively, an air conditioner may only cost $2,000, or $170 a year, but could add $10 to the weekly rent return of a property in far north Queensland, and additional tax breaks when you depreciate that air conditioner.

Remember, if you are a long-term property investor, you are not looking to add value to achieve a higher sales price – you are after more rent. While adding value may give you a higher valuation which allows you to leverage into more property, if cash flow is your problem today you are probably not in a position to buy more property anyway, and so the ability to increase value becomes a moot point for the short term.

Increase rents and have shorter term leases

This may sound like I am stating the obvious, but I often meet many investors who are either too busy to keep their eye on market rent, are relying on their property manager to suggest rental increases, or do not want to upset what they perceive as a good tenant by increasing the rent.

Many parts of Australia are in the midst of great pressure on rent returns. For some years now, values have increased in unprecedented amounts in many areas, and rental yields have been left behind. After a period of sustained values growth, rental yields will also follow and experience a wave of pressure. If you add to that our current housing afford-ability crisis, and our alarming undersupply of housing, a fact which is being exacerbated by the inability of developers to access funding to build, then it is clear that pretty soon, people will be almost fighting in the streets to rent a property. It is likely that the current rent you are asking on your property is already out of date and an increase is easily achievable.

In addition, under such circumstances, be sure to keep all of your leases short term, usually around six months only. During these times when there are more tenants available than properties to house them, it is crucial that you keep up with the market. Locking a tenant into a longer term lease, no matter how good you perceive them to be, will mean that you will miss out on the frequent opportunity to increase rents and so ease your own cash flow issues.

For those of you who feel a responsibility toward a good tenant who you have had for years, now is not the time to be overly benevolent. By all means, allow them some privileges, but don't charge under-market rent. Times are tough and keeping rents so low that you experience cash flow problems could mean that it becomes a case of you or the tenant – and it will most likely be you. There are a lot of good tenants around at the moment, and your job in this world is not to be worrying about cash flow management for your tenant.

Spend less

Start in your own back yard. Examine your budgets and see where you can make cuts. It is during tough economic times that those who stick with budgeting and investing become the most successful. In the olden days, where positive cash flow property was abundant, investing in property was easy. You could buy anywhere and do well, and many properties were positive cash flow, meaning that you had no commitment from your own pocket. Now that the yields are down, property investing has once again become difficult and only those with a desire to get ahead will see the opportunities which presently abound.

If, on the other hand, your cash flow is so tight that you are not able to meet your current commitments, then it could be time to sell. Be aware that to do so you will need to have a reasonable expectation of what you can achieve as a sales price, and you will be exiting a market which many others are exiting at the same time. Selling will be difficult unless you are prepared to take a lower price than anyone else. If you do manage to sell, and you exit the investment with cash left over, use it to immediately reduce your other commitments, so the time at which you can reinvest comes sooner. Resist the temptation to reward yourself with a holiday or new car and make your commitment to achieve a better financial situation complete by minimising debt wherever possible.

For those determined to stay in the market, remember you may be now facing a temporary period of low cash flows on property and it is time for you to make some sacrifices if you wish to be successful over the long term. Tighten your belt and increase your commitment to your future financial security. Do anything you can to avoid selling because the situation is already easing every day and you do not want to look back and wish you had tried harder to hang on to an asset which may have one day provided a comfortable future for you.

KEY POINTS

- ~ During difficult times, you can boost cash flows in a number of ways.
- ~ You should claim your tax deductions weekly in your pay.
- ~ Talk to your property manager about whether adding value will result in a rental increase.
- ~ Look at your own budget and do all you can to hang onto your property through the hard times.

11

PORTFOLIO MANAGEMENT

If you have already commenced your property portfolio, chances are you will have many questions about what to do next. Every day I answer dozens of queries from people at various stages of their investing, and many of them are unaware that it is just as important to manage the portfolio itself as it is to manage each property.

Portfolio management is about reviewing and revising what you have. Set and forget may be the main theme, however there may be times when you must look over what you have, consider if everything you own is performing as it should, and decide if it should stay in the portfolio. This is just as important with one property as it is with many.

From all of the queries I do receive, here are some of the more common issues that have been raised, and my suggestions for managing them.

Poorly performing property

One of the greatest fears that most property investors have is that they will buy a property which will be a complete lemon and in doing so they will become financially ruined. It's quite unlikely that the outcome of such a purchase will actually financially ruin you – the worst case scenario is usually a forced sale at lower than was paid, leaving a residual debt which increases your monthly home loan repayment, or a need to lower rent and take a lower cash flow that must be subsidised from your own pocket.

Having said that, if you have purchased a property which isn't performing, you need to address it and take action. It's no use allowing it to just sit in your portfolio. If it is truly a bad property, it will only get worse and more money will be lost each day that you hold it.

To establish whether that property is an actual lemon, here are some characteristics of property lemons:

~ More than eight weeks a year vacancy for standard residential property, and if you have purchased a serviced apartment, hotel or other niche market property, less occupancy than you need to pay your costs for the property.
~ A value which is less than you paid for it, which is still going backwards AND a very low cash flow.
~ Situated in an ugly duckling suburb that you thought might be turning around, but you realise subsequently you may have been wrong – it is always being vandalised by the tenants or others, meaning it costs you more money in repair bills than it gives you in income.

What *is* notably excluded from the list above are properties which aren't growing and those with low or negative cash flow. Lack of growth and negative cash flow only becomes an issue if it in some way prevents you from adding to your

PORTFOLIO MANAGEMENT | 171

portfolio. It is perfectly acceptable to have in your portfolio a property or two which are not performing at the present time, as long as they still show characteristics which point to economic vibrancy.

If you have ascertained that you might indeed have purchased a property which is either never going to perform suitably, or which is holding you back from entering the market in an area which is vibrant, then here is what you should do.

1. Assess the true financial impact of that property upon you today

If you just don't like that property, or it's annoying you in some way but there is no other financial impact, there is no point rushing into a sale.

On the other hand, if it is impacting upon your ability to meet your personal expenses or otherwise enjoy your life now, or its existence in your portfolio limits your capacity to borrow again to buy something else somewhere that may be about to become a hotspot, you must sell. Don't make the mistake of hanging onto it, hoping for that elusive capital gain, or because you believe that you have to try to recoup your losses. Although property markets do go in cycles, these cycles are measured and expressed as an average only. This means that within these cycles, a property in any one area can still stay in a trough indefinitely and behave very differently to the average.

It will be hard to do, but you must sell the property and cut your losses. You will be able to carry forward this loss indefinitely to offset any future capital gains and the sale will halt further loss.

2. Consider keeping it a while longer

If the reason you consider it to be a lemon is because it is suffering from value losses, but its cash flow is still positive or at a minimal negative amount, you may want to keep it for a while longer.

I have found that, with some exceptions, many properties which seem to be losing value are doing so because too much was paid for them in the first place. Make sure that this is not your situation. Did you pay market value, or, if you bought from a developer, might there have been commissions which boosted the purchase price over market value? Before selling due to a loss in value, get hold of a copy of my book *The 20 Must Ask Questions® for Every Property Investor* (Wiley) and ask my 20 Questions® again. Examine the economic landscape, because the last thing you will want is to sell that property just before a boom.

If it is your only investment, and you have decided to keep the property, be sure to double your efforts at debt elimination so you can still create equity and leverage again.

3. Sell now and get straight back into the market

If you are experiencing a crippling negative cash flow, and the area shows distinct signs that growth is light-years away, you may be best to sell now and get straight back into the market with a property purchased in an area with greater economic potential.

4. Sell and cut your losses

If you have a property which attracts unsavoury tenants and your landlord's insurance policy has reached its maximum allowable claims, this may again be a good reason to sell and cut your losses. Where one property takes up the bulk of your time and energies, it may be better out of your portfolio.

What do I do when I get to retirement?

All good investment plans include an exit strategy. This is what I learned as I studied to become a financial adviser.

The truth is I secretly disagree! In the time I have been advising on both property and other investments, there have been so many changes to legislation and so many new products and services come onto the market that anyone with a set exit strategy has probably changed it at least a dozen times by now!

When my husband and I started our property portfolio, the plan was to get to retirement, sell half to reduce the debt, and live off the remaining income from the rest. Now that seems like a silly idea. As we head toward our retirement years, we are paying off debt and gaining considerable equity in the portfolio. The greater the equity, the higher the cash flow, because as rents are generally a percentage of values, the income on our portfolio increases while our interest costs decrease. By the time we retire the difference between what comes in and what goes out should be great enough to provide a retirement income without needing to sell. I now realise that if I can hang on to all of the properties, my exposure to a growth market will be greater, and as I get older the values will just keep growing. Ten years after I retire the cash flows should be higher again, even if I pay no more off the debt or add to the portfolio.

> The greater the equity, the higher the cash flow...

The other positive is that rental income is accepted by the bank for serviceability on a loan so I may even be able to continue to borrow to buy more properties.

And so the point is, while you may have a general idea of how you will exit your portfolio, my advice is to not set it in concrete. You must base the ultimate decision on rules and regulations when the time comes and upon what you want as a lifestyle when you reach retirement.

What is the value of the property portfolio I will need?

If you have ever been to an investment or wealth creation seminar, you've probably heard all the platitudes, just as I have. People who want to sell something to you will spout all of the facts and figures about poverty in retirement, designed to frighten you into taking action there and then.

In truth, just as we all have different incomes today, and enjoy and want different lifestyles, the goal we all aim for as a retirement income will differ too. When I am asked how much property is needed to retire well, I will usually use as my benchmark the current aged pension, extrapolated out to present a figure at the time that person wishes to retire. If this amount is used as a base to represent the minimum income that someone can achieve by doing nothing, goals can be set as to how far past this minimum income one would like to go.

Let's assume a period of 10 years. By then, I'd say that the average couple aged pension will sit at around $25,000 per annum.

Over 10 years, a basic portfolio of four properties, purchased at $250,000 each and increasing in value at 5% per year would provide equity which exceeded debt by about $550,000. At 5% return, this would provide an income of $27,500, which just about matches that pension. A couple with investment income of that amount would likely still qualify for the full amount of the pension too, since the government does allow some income to be earned, tax free, without it impacting on the pension. As such, a couple with four properties would be earning a total income of about $52,500, most probably tax free.

Of course, unless you purchased all of the properties in year one, which some are not able to do, you would not always be able to buy property for just $250,000, as the price of even the lowest end property will rise over this period. But all things are relative and as the prices rise, so does the amount by which the properties appreciate each year.

Each extra year that an investor can add to this scenario past 10 years improves the outcome considerably, since the growth compounds. Each property added will also improve the overall outcome too, as a greater exposure to that growth occurs when the asset base is wider.

If you also considered that, in any ten-year cycle, there are likely to be some higher than average growth rates, then $52,500 per year becomes the absolute minimum a person would expect as an income from this strategy, with much higher incomes the greater likelihood.

Most people can comfortably achieve a $1,000,000 net worth in a ten-year period.

My experience is that most people can comfortably achieve a $1,000,000 net worth in a ten-year period – resulting in a $50,000 (plus any allowable pension) income if invested with a conservative 5% return – and many people will significantly exceed this modest forecast.

Should I sell a property after the big capital gain has occurred?

In the beginning of this book, I referred to market timing. I wanted to point out how, with the right amount of forecasting and research, it was possible to improve market timing. If that's the situation, then this will mean that, most of the time, you will be buying in areas which are about to enter a phase of growth which outperforms the average.

The question then becomes one of asking whether a property should be sold after a large gain, to enable the process to be repeated again.

The answer is yes, and no. Or possibly!

In fact there is no blanket response to this question, but there are factors you can consider to make the choice:

~ If your research indicates that you may have purchased in an area which experienced growth from extrinsic growth drivers, and you can see no other influences on the horizon, then you might consider a sale before too many other properties come on the market, or vacancies grow too high.

~ As with the lemon property we discussed earlier, if holding that property means that you are unable to borrow to buy something else which has yet to have its boom, then a sale might be considered.

~ If that property is now settling down to its 'stabilised' growth phase, and still shows signs that it can now sustain at least average growth rates, then I suggest holding it.

Importantly, you must do the financial calculations before making any decisions. If you have made a really good gain, capital gains tax may make selling a bad idea. Always remember that unrealised gains are far more valuable to you than realised gains. If the property can sit in your portfolio and not hamper further leveraging, that may be the best idea.

How much should I spend on each property?

How much you spend when buying a property depends upon how much you have to pay to buy it!

When you uncover an area with great potential, it is likely that it will have yields of around 5%. This is because rental yields decrease *after* values growth has occurred, and high rental yields are often an indicator of an area which is on the cusp of achieving some good growth.

Therefore, when you find the right area, and you have established that it has all of the features of a secure and growing investment, then you should pay the market price for a property.

If the market price means that the property is out of your price range, then you cannot buy in that area. You will need to find another suitable area with lower buy-in prices that you can afford.

I'm quite confident that this is unlikely to occur though. This is because I have yet to find a potential hotspot which carries price-tags out of the affordability range of most investors. If an area has high buy-in prices, then it has already had its major growth phase and is either a cold-spot, or an area in its stabilised growth phase, and you should not be buying there anyway.

How do I manage my capital gains tax (CGT) liability?

Since property is an investment, you are liable to pay capital gains tax on any realised gain in the same way as a share or managed fund investor. How much tax you pay, and using which method, depends upon when the property was purchased.

For the purposes of this book, we will assume that you have not bought a property yet. You are not likely to be reading a book such as this after you already have all of the properties you need in your portfolio, unless it is to feel remorseful about all the ways you have gone wrong!

Therefore you will pay capital gains tax in one of two ways.

1. If the property has been held for more than 12 months, and it has been purchased in your own name(s), you will receive a 50% discount on the gain. The purchase price and the sale price are both adjusted to take into account allowable buying and selling costs, and the difference is halved. This is then added to your income for the year and you pay tax at your highest marginal rate of tax.

2. If the property has been held for less than 12 months then there is no discount and you must account for the entire gain.

Capital gains tax is a cost of investing that must be accounted for in your calculations. You can lessen the impact of CGT by timing the sale of property wherever possible. This may include selling property in years when you have a lower income – such as after you have left the paid workforce – or by staggering the sales over a number of years so that you don't report a huge gain all in the one year.

Remember too that any capital losses you may be carrying forward can be accounted to offset capital gain.

Review and revise

As with any investment, your portfolio needs constant reviewing and revising. You must keep track of rents so that you know when to increase them. You must track your income and expenses so that you can satisfy your responsibilities to the tax office. And you must constantly assess the performance of each individual property, to ensure that it both remains a viable investment, and sits comfortably within your portfolio. Set and forget is important in terms of not dwelling on a single purchase and moving on to the next one, but a constant review of all of your properties is most important to ensure that your portfolio is always as strong as it can possibly be.

Constant review of all of your properties is most important.

KEY POINTS

~ You must constantly review and revise your portfolio to ensure it remains valid and appropriate.

~ Evaluate that poorly performing property before selling to ensure that it really doesn't belong in your portfolio.

~ Your exit strategy should remain flexible, as many things can change between now and the time when you will need to live off your property portfolio.

~ Selling after a big capital gain may not be the best option.

~ Unrealised gains may be worth more to you than realised gains.

~ The number of properties you need depends upon how much more than an aged pension you would like to achieve.

~ How much should be spent on each property depends upon your personal risk profile and budget.

~ Being aware of the capital gains tax regime of the day is important for all investors.

NEGOTIATING

Once you have done all of the required research and chosen the right area – and you are sure that you have considered the area which is the best possible one at that moment in time, which matches your own appetite for risk – it's time to begin negotiations on actual properties that you find.

From my experience, buyers seem to be divided into three main groups; those who never negotiate, as if the listed price were a set price, those who negotiate but know that they do so ineffectively, and those who believe that they are good negotiators, all of the time. In truth, I have found that the last category, those who believe that they negotiate well, can be further divided into those who *think* they negotiate well and those who actually *do* negotiate well, with those negotiating well only making up the smaller proportion.

Many people believe that negotiation is about starting, say 5 to 10% under the asking price, and meeting the vendor halfway. This may seem like a win/win situation, but such an approach is relying on the vendor having asked for a price slightly above actual market value, and a buyer starting slightly below market value. In reality, this is rarely the case, and the result is usually that the buyer pays over market value once negotiations are complete.

...the result is usually that the buyer pays over market value once negotiations are complete.

A client of mine, Lindsay, had a property for which he had paid $500,000, following some poor advice he had received prior to meeting with us. The property was a typical sea-view property, and this is what had attracted Lindsay to it in the first place – the mistaken belief that coastal property qualified as a good investment purely because of its location.

A year later it became painfully obvious that this property needed to go, as it was frequently vacant and its value seemed to be rapidly declining. The property was placed on the market for the original purchase price of $500,000, and there it sat for some time.

A few months later, a buyer who fancied himself as a shrewd negotiator commenced negotiations, offering $450,000. The two met at $475,000 and, on the surface, it looked like Lindsay had come out of this badly, having lost $25,000 plus his costs, while the buyer had a significant win, buying this property at less than Lindsay had paid for it.

The reality was that Lindsay was the clear winner in this case – the true market value of that property when Lindsay sold it was closer to $440,000. Luckily for Lindsay, the buyer had done little research and in fact there was little movement in this market at all for him to use as a comparison. However, more careful due diligence by this buyer would have revealed how much he should have paid. He would have been able to discover that prices were in freefall in this area, and clever enquiry may have even revealed that Lindsay really needed to sell this property, giving any buyer much more power in this transaction than Lindsay could have.

I know that Lindsay would have taken less than was paid, and in this transaction several mistakes were made. The point to note here is that buying a property is not like buying a watch in Bali – there, you know to start at around 20% of any price and meet at about 50%. When you negotiate for a property, there is not a single rule or method which needs to be followed. How you negotiate, and how far below asking price you pay, depends on a number of factors which are occurring at that moment.

Commencing negotiations

Before you even begin to haggle over price, you have to uncover as many facts as possible about the property itself, the market value and the people selling it.

When I find a property that I like, I never make an offer straight up. I phone the listing agent and try to get them into some kind of general conversation. My aim here is to relax the agent and see what I can find out about the property, and its owners.

After a general chit chat, the kinds of questions I will ask include:

~ How long has the property been on the market for, including the length of time any other agency has had the listing?

~ If this were your property, what would you do to it to make it rentable?

~ Are you or the vendors aware of any defect that may require me to make repairs within the first few years?

~ Why is the vendor selling?

~ Are there time-limiting factors in the sale and will the vendor reduce more quickly to sell?

~ Is a quick sale advantageous to the vendor?

~ What are the vendors doing after they make this sale?

~ How many other offers have been made on this property?

~ How many inspections have taken place so far?

By law, an agent is supposed to answer all of your questions with the truth, but you can't always be sure that this will be the case. To maximise the chances that I am actually getting some element of truth, I always tell the agent at the outset that I am making notes about their answers, just in case I need to refer back to them at a later stage. This way, I don't need to warn them against lying to me because the inference is that I will not hesitate to take action should I find out later that I was in some way misled by untruthful answers.

Another way to achieve this result, and still have a written record of the responses, is to key in such questions and email them to the agent. This works where time is on your side, but in a warm or hot market, many agents simply won't bother to respond.

> By law, an agent is supposed to answer all of your questions with the truth.

Once I have answers, I will usually wait a few days before I make an offer. The purpose behind waiting is to simply place the power where I want it to stay – that is, with me! Anytime a buyer seems too eager, they forfeit an element of power and allow the other party to sit in the box seat.

Attitude

Negotiation is as much about attitude as it is about getting the numbers right at the outset. Having the right attitude will do two things for you:

1. It will give you the power in the negotiations, as you will appear to have the most strength and resilience.

2. It will allow you to remain unemotional and to walk away from a transaction which is not going well. This way, you will not over-pay and later regret your actions.

The problem with property is that its very physical nature tends to invite an emotional attachment, even when you think you are remaining detached. I know this all too well. Despite my claim that I am a veritable emotional desert when it comes to buying property, this is not actually true. Like most buyers, once I have found a property, I tend to visualise owning it – how great it is going to look in my portfolio. Having viewed pictures, I've probably been guilty of choosing based on a physical attraction to that property too, and this is where the emotional attachment really begins to form.

To counter this, I do two things. Firstly I *always* have more than one property which I am negotiating on at any one time. This has the effect of not only giving me a suitable alternative, so that I do not become too attached to one property, but it also adds an element of urgency to the negotiations from the seller's perspective. While I don't try to play off one vendor against another, having a second and third choice allows me to place a time limit on the negotiations of each. Communicating this to the agent also places a time limit on how quickly they must consult with their vendor.

So, exactly what is the right attitude? Quite simply, it is the attitude that, if negotiations fail, it won't matter to you. There will be another deal, most likely a better one, around the corner. The purpose of the failed deal is simply to sharpen your negotiation skills so that you are even more effective in future transactions.

You must be totally separated from the property, emotionally, and you must view each and every negotiation as a step toward the right property, even if those particular negotiations fail. That way, it will be much easier for you to walk away and move on. An inability to do this may result in paying over the market value for a property. This may not be a bad thing, where the market is heating up quickly and you promptly reclaim any lost equity through immediate growth.

> There will be another deal, most likely a better one, around the corner.

But, if you have purchased a property in its pre-hotspot phase, you may wait a while before values shift. Paying more than you need to for a property may result in a longer timeframe between purchases, and if this happens more than once you may well slow up acquisition of property as you struggle to regain the equity lost in that bad negotiation. It will be far better to wait a few weeks for the next property upon which you successfully negotiate, than pay too much for a property and start well behind.

Your first bid

Once you have set the scene via a self-assured conversation with the agent, in which you have asserted yourself as a knowledgeable and confident buyer, you need to prepare your first bid.

Depending upon the state in which you are buying, this can occur in a number of ways, however it never needs to be as complicated as some agents will have you believe.

As I write this, I am negotiating on a property in Queensland. We are at a stalemate, with the vendor on $229,000 and me at $220,000. I am confident that I am at market value with this, my final bid, having arrived at $220,000 after starting at $210,000. The vendors have only moved by $1,000, and that alone is enough to make me walk away in disgust, as they are simply not entering into the spirit of it all!

The agent continues to tell me that her poor 'young' vendors *need* $230,000 to enable them to upgrade to a property they have found. While I can feel some sympathy for these sellers (most of it for the fact that their agent is failing to guide them well), their youth and their needs are not my problem. The agent tells me they don't *really* want to sell their property, (I guess that explains why it is on the market??), and if they don't get $229,000, they will take it off the market (again, not my problem!).

It's been on the market for almost three months and in that time there has not been a single bid, and virtually no attendance at the frequent 'home opens'. I know this to be true because I call the agent after every home open and I ask her questions:

"How did it go?" is usually met with "Very well, thank you".

"Exactly how many people were there?"

"How many took a contract?"

"How many left you their phone numbers?"

These are questions which are harder to brush off, and I remind this agent that I am writing this all down.

In fact, there are hundreds of other properties listed in the same price bracket as this property, many of them cheaper, albeit in need of some upgrade, which has already occurred in this property.

My research *and* the fact that this property has failed to attract any kind of other attention reveals to me that I am more than likely on the money with my final bid. I'll probably get it, but not until these vendors waste a little more money on loan interest as they finally realise that they are asking too much. Worse still for the vendor is that one of my other bids may eventuate at the same time that they decide to take my offer, and they will have lost the sale.

...a formal, written offer, contained in an email, is sufficient to commence negotiations.

When I made my initial bid, it was in an email. It was written formally, outlining my terms and conditions, and providing a date by which the offer needed to be accepted. The offer referred also to the fact that I would be negotiating on another property after that date, but that I would see this offer through before making other offers. Rather than make all of the offers at once, this method, I think, is the most fair and open.

The agent responded that my offer would have more power, and be taken more seriously, if it was included as part of a purchase contract. Now, this is a ridiculous suggestion, and this was the point at which this agent and I purloined for the upper hand.

I countered that, as the offer was in writing, it must be

presented to the vendor and that signing a contract (which would bind me immediately if the offer was accepted) would in no way increase the seriousness of my offer. I suggested that it would be the skill of the agent which would assist the vendors to realise the seriousness, rather than the paper it was written on.

To that end, regardless of the accepted norm in any state, a formal, written offer, contained in an email, is sufficient to commence negotiations. More formal contracts and offers can be signed once the deal is sealed.

When you make your first bid, consider the following.

Your first bid should *never* be your final offer

A first bid cannot be so low as to be ridiculous and alienate the vendor from entering the negotiations. As such, your first bid should never be your final offer, even if you suggest that it is. If you make your final offer up front, and the vendor rejects it outright, you have no room to move.

Negotiate in small chunks

Most vendors, if they are genuinely wishing to sell, will in all likelihood take less than they think they will. The point here is that they won't immediately meet a very low offer, but if they can be encouraged down slowly, in very small chunks, they may end up taking less than they thought they would. It's a subtle, mental thing, but moving in small degrees such as this makes the vendor feel they are only giving away a thousand or two, rather than a big chunk of say, $20,000.

Meet at market value

The aim is not to meet in the middle, it's to meet at market value. You must be very sure of market value and have evidence by way of recent sales in the area of similar style and sized homes. Sometimes a vendor is a long way from market value and it will take a considerable number of bids to bring them lower. At other times, they may be very close to that market value and so negotiations should be swift. In any event, your first bid must always be *under* market value so that you can eventually land on it, or better still snag a bargain.

Consider the extras

A little trick which can sometimes work is to build into your offer a request for additional items which you can later drop. This is not always possible, especially if you have not viewed the property and are not sure what it contains, but we have used this trick once in the past.

We were negotiating on an owner-occupied property and our first bid, which was actually $200,000 under the asking price, included a request to leave the double fridge, the custom-made wall units, the outdoor barbecue and a bunch of other items.

We actually didn't want those things, but our first few bids involved letting go of them rather than moving on price. As the vendor dropped in lots of $30,000, we dropped off the extra items, one at a time! In the end we moved $50,000 only in price, but gave up the extras. The point is that the vendors felt like they were winning as we let go of these items.

Once you have submitted your first offer, in writing, it's a waiting game. Remember, you must include a timeframe for the acceptance or rejection of the bid, or else the power will shift back to the agent and their vendor. Don't sit around and wait for their offer though. Keep looking around and working on your first bids on other properties so that you can be ready to go if this one falls through.

What's in the offer?

The offer should include:

~ Your bid

~ The terms and conditions. For example:

 - A subject to finance clause, including the total amount you will be seeking and the lender you will be seeking it from. This way if your preferred lender and amount is not approved you cannot be forced to try elsewhere;

 - Subject to pest and building inspections, and a resulting report which does not require you to spend money on even minor repairs;

 - Subject to the offer being accepted by a set time and date, as defined by you;

 - Any other special conditions which you would like met before going ahead – such as an agreement to make a repair, have a formal valuation confirming price, etc.

 - The reason for the amount you have offered – supporting information is really important in this section. You should list recent comparative sales, defects in the property which should result in a reduction to the price, the costs of any renovations you will need to undertake, and any other evidence to suggest that your price is closer to market value than theirs.

Sign the offer and include the names which you would like the final contracts to include. This way, such an offer represents a formal bid and must be presented to the vendor.

Subsequent offers

Be sure that all subsequent offers proceed exactly as the first – in writing. If the agent calls to reject your bid or provide a counter offer, ask that it be sent to you in writing. This has the subtle effect of making sure everything is concrete and it makes for smoother negotiations.

Your aim is to be the one who is making the final bid. It is for this reason that you should only ever raise your offer by small amounts, and taper off the concessions to your increments so that they become smaller each time. This way the vendor will realise you are coming to the end of your capacity to increase your bid, and they will not wait for a greater increase that isn't going to come.

Your aim is to be the one who is making the final bid.

Here's an example.

Corey wrote to me a while ago to tell me of his recent successful negotiations. He had offered $280,000 on a $325,000 property. His second bid, placed a few hours after his first in a response to the vendor's counter of $320,000, was $290,000 and, when he had not heard for two days from the agent, he upped this to $300,000. The vendor countered at $310,000 and Corey accepted this.

I believe Corey could have paid just $300,000 for this property. He should have waited a full 24 to 48 hours after receiving that first counter bid from the vendor, just to make them a little nervous. He then should have responded with a bid of $285,000 and then, after again waiting a few days and receiving another vendor offer, countered at $290,000. If this was played well, at that stage the vendor may have already lowered their price to $310,000, at which time Corey could have started bidding in smaller amounts of $2,000, then $1,000.

The point here is that the negotiations continue, even if each party is only moving in small increments. When bids continue to be made it is more likely the vendor will end up lower than they had originally intended. It's crucial that your bids are made in very small amounts and, as you get closer to the vendor, slow down the frequency.

Ensure it is you who is making the final bid. In Corey's case, the final vendor bid of $310,000 should have been met at least by a final buyer offer of, say, $308,000.

What if the vendor will not negotiate?

Where a vendor refuses to negotiate, you should also refuse to continue. Move on to the second and third properties you have on the list. Remember, a vendor will always ask for more than they will take and their refusal to at least enter the negotiations should result in their loss of you as a potential

It's crucial that your bids are made in very small amounts...

buyer. Keep an eye on that property and you'll see the listed price reduced sometime soon.

Vendors often say that they would have taken less than was paid for their property, while buyers usually say that they paid more than they originally intended. This is an indication that few people truly negotiate well.

While knowing what motivates the seller is important,

your most powerful tool in negotiating is a thorough knowledge of true market value. You may not always be able to discover what is motivating the seller. The current listed price of other properties can't tell you this – only an investigation of what has recently sold and how it compares to the property you are looking at can give you an accurate guideline of where to start.

And remember to keep the ball in your court at all times, by having the last word and by remaining calm and detached. It can be fun to negotiate when you do it well, and the outcome of successful negotiations can be very satisfying indeed.

~ Find out as much as you can about the vendor: why they are selling, what are their timeframes, have they found another property yet, are they willing to negotiate?

~ Find out as much as you can about the property: how long has it been on the market, how much needs to be spent on it, is it tenant ready, how much will it fetch as a rental, what are the recent sales prices of similar properties?

~ Ask for more than you expect or want – if possible add items which you are prepared to release in your negotiations, so that you can make concessions which are not necessarily about price.

~ Never take the first counter offer.

~ Never increase your bids in large amounts.

~ Never split the difference.

~ Only 'meet in the middle' if the middle is fair market value.

~ Taper your bids – as you get higher, make the increments smaller and less frequent.

~ If you are asked by the agent 'what is your maximum price' *never*, under any circumstances, answer that question. *Never* indicate anything about what you are prepared to pay, or what you can borrow, even if you think you are suggesting a low amount. If it's accepted, you'll kick yourself for not suggesting an even lower amount.

~ Always move in small amounts but keep the offers flowing to continuously engage the vendor.

~ Leave all emotion out of the transaction.

13

THOSE PSYCHOLOGICAL BARRIERS

The biggest enemy of many property investors is themselves. Just as we must ensure that, financially, we have sufficient security to obtain, and maintain, a property portfolio, many of us need to do some work on our mindset so that we can freely and successful buy property.

If you are buying alone, this is a little easier. If you don't get over the mental barriers which are holding you back, you only have yourself to blame!

Where you are buying with a partner of some kind, it's more difficult. I often see a clear mismatch in the attitudes and goals of couples who I meet on their investment journey. This kind of disconnect can be very stressful and really get in the way of a successful outcome.

The biggest enemy that many property investors have is themselves.

Often, after agreeing that owning a property portfolio is a desired investment strategy, couples or individuals can have great difficulty taking the action required to make it happen. Many of them spend time and money getting the right education and support, and still fail to get off square one. As they procrastinate, the years keep rolling on and I always know that, without doubt, they will look back and regret that they didn't take the chance when they could have.

Many years ago a couple consulted with us about their future. They had paid off their own modest home, and both had jobs, albeit quite low paying ones. Many of their friends had begun to work on a wealth accumulation plan to allow for a better retirement, and so they felt compelled to follow the crowd.

We structured a personal strategy for them, and all that was left was for them to make the property selection with which they were the most comfortable. On no less than four occasions, a property was found, negotiated upon and contracts drawn up. Then they would suddenly pull out of the deal after a weekend of angst, headaches and endless questioning about 'what if?'

> It is the psychological factors which become the barriers that prevent many people from achieving investing success.

After a long session with the couple, I ascertained two things. Firstly, they were attempting to embrace a strategy which was foreign to them, simply because other people said they should, not because they were truly committed themselves. Secondly, they were in a financial comfort zone, being debt free, and had a fear of debt which was blocking their vision for the future.

We addressed these issues by first of all establishing what the future might look like if they did nothing, and then working out if this picture of the future fulfilled all of their goals. We discovered that, in fact, their present course of action would not allow for them to enjoy one of the basic goals they had always held dear – to buy a caravan and tour the country. In formulating and then painting the picture for this goal, the couple were able to see that taking no action would result in this goal becoming an impossibility, and that the action to be taken did not involve unacceptable risk. They didn't need to build a portfolio of dozens of properties, which was definitely outside of their comfort zone due to the debt level required, and a few well chosen inexpensive properties would probably be enough. We also established that, since going into debt again was also a barrier, they should start small with a very cheap property and build from there.

This couple now hold nine properties in their portfolio and are looking for more. Having started the process, and then subsequently discovering that none of their fears materialised, they gained confidence and now even enjoy the process. And their goal for the caravan is well and truly back on the agenda.

In all of the years I have been assisting people to buy property, I have discovered that all of the knowledge in the world can still do very little for most people. It is the psychological factors which become the barriers that prevent many people from achieving investing success. Knowing what these factors are, and then identifying your own personal psychological barriers, so that you can remove them, is the most important first step to take as an investor.

Fear

The first factor usually holding people back from moving ahead with their property portfolio is fear. This fear comes in a range of disguises. Here are the main ones, along with some strategies for overcoming them.

Fear of losing your own home

If you have already achieved a comfortable debt level, and have considerable equity in your own home, you may worry that making the wrong choice will lead to financial ruin. In past chapters, I have shown that the likelihood of this is very small and this fear must be put into perspective.

To recap, here is another example to demonstrate how illogical this fear really is.

> Imagine you own a home worth $300,000 and you owe $150,000. You buy a property for $200,000 using a debt of $210,000 (to include buying costs) secured across your own home and the new property. Your debt is now $360,000, and your equity has been reduced, for now, by $10,000 down to $140,000.

> For any number of reasons, it all goes horribly wrong and you are forced to sell the new property. To do this quickly you must reduce the price, and you only achieve $180,000. Now you have a debt of $180,000 which is $30,000 more than you had when you started.

> This is far from ideal, but it also is unlikely that an extra $30,000 of debt (which would cost you a net of $40 a week) will force you to lose the home you already had.

To deal with this fear, work out the worst case scenario and ask yourself if you can afford that outcome. If not, then you should not buy, but it is more likely that the worst thing to come out of a failed property investment is an increased personal debt that you probably can manage. And remember, the actual likelihood of this result is relatively small.

...work out the worst case scenario and ask yourself if you can afford that outcome.

Fear that you will not be able to afford to repay the debt if the property is vacant

When people first begin to consider this possibility, they imagine that there could be months in which no income is received and they will be required to meet the mortgage repayments from their own pocket. If this is your fear, you must consider:

1. If you buy property in the cash flow phase of its cycle, you will better be able to manage those periods of vacancy, as the property is either costing you very little, or giving you additional income each week which can be saved for those rainy days. For example, a property with a $20 a week positive cash flow gives you a total of $1,040 a year, which, for a property renting at $200 a week, provides five weeks of allowable vacancy before you must even reach into your pocket.

2. Tax deductions reduce your shortfall. So, technically, for every $200 a week that you do not receive, a taxpayer in the 30% bracket will receive an additional $60 tax break, reducing your commitment to $140, or allowing more weeks of vacancy

3. In reality, if a property is vacant for a week or two, you can take action then by reducing the rent. Even if you reduced a $200 a week rent to $180, you would only be losing $20 a week ($14 after tax breaks) and you will have boosted your chances of attracting a tenant as you have become more competitive.

4. For vacancy caused by an inability to rent out a damaged property, you should be sure to have landlord's insurance. At an after-tax cost of around $7 a week, this is vital.

From this you can see that there are many ways to deal with vacancy issues, and it is highly unlikely that your property will need to remain vacant for long enough to cause financial stress to you.

Fear of making the wrong choice

Buying a property involves making a large purchase. Even if you borrow all of the money and use little or none of your own, your commitment is a big one. Why is it, then, that people so carelessly choose property, using all manner of emotional reasons to buy? Investors mistakenly believe they can use a 'gut feeling' about property, or base their choices around what they would personally like to live in. Worse still, they follow the crowds, take advice from their unqualified friends, buy a property in their dream location near the beach and largely put faith in people who have a vested interest in their purchase – such as the person selling the property. It's no wonder so many bad choices are made.

> Investors mistakenly believe they can use a 'gut feeling' about property.

You can never remove all of the risk when you invest in property, but you can manage it and increase the chances that what you buy will work out well. However, you can only do this by becoming educated first. The reason I developed the 20 Must Ask Questions® was to provide a benchmark which becomes the minimum criteria that a property and area must display before it becomes likely to perform well. If your fear is that you will choose badly, then leave your emotions at home, learn how to invest well and arm yourself with my 20 Must Ask Questions®. Then, commit to only buying property which can satisfy them.

Procrastination

Every year I attend the property expos held all over the country. And every year it seems the same people approach me to tell me that they heard my presentation last year. They had felt inspired but then after they got home they simply could not bring themselves to get started. They admit to thinking about it a lot, but the action never seems to occur.

If you know that you have the capacity to buy property, and you also have a desire somewhere deep inside to do so but you never take the step, you must recognise that you are a procrastinator. The worst thing for procrastinators is that they usually experience very deep feelings of remorse when they miss the boat and realise at a later date that they had the capacity to get ahead, but missed it.

Start to take control of your life by scheduling the tasks which must be completed.

If you are a procrastinator, then you must develop the habit of writing down your goals, developing the steps required to achieve them and then putting these steps as a must-do on your calendar. Devise penalties for yourself if you don't meet the date set and rewards if you do. Start to take control of your life by scheduling the tasks which must be completed in this way and soon you will own an investment property.

Lacking motivation and time

So, you go to a seminar, read a book and you are buzzing with excitement about the property portfolio you are about to build.

You go home, and the next day when you wake up the kids are sick, the boss wants you to do overtime and your mother-in-law has come for a two-week visit. Suddenly it all becomes too hard and as each day passes, buying property slips way down on your list of priorities. Regardless of how much education or desire you have, life easily gets in the way, and before you know it, another year has passed and you are a year closer to retirement.

People are amazed at the number of properties I own, and figure it is because I have special knowledge, or skills. The truth of the matter is that I spend as much time as I can in the 'property headspace', so that I am always exposed to new learning. In my case I own more property than most because every day, from the moment I arrive at my desk, I am working with property. I am answering questions, motivating others and even if I wanted to, I could not get away from it. It's no wonder that all I ever want to do is buy more!

Two years ago I examined Destiny® clients to work out why some were more successful than others. I wanted to know why, since they all had access to the same information from us, and since we had established before they became a client that they were financially able to succeed, some did amazingly well and others either plodded or did not buy any property at all.

It came down to one simple thing – those clients who attended every event we offered, came to property focus group sessions, made consistent appointments for one-to-one support sessions with us, used all of the property tracking tools we provided and did every single thing we suggested were those who had the greatest success. The reason for this is that they are the ones who were consistently placing themselves in what I call the 'property headspace' – a place where the motivation continues on an almost daily basis and results in a constant focus on the end goal. When you live in that space, you can't help but buy property!

Allowing life to get in the way is no excuse. I have five children, a national business, two TV shows and I write books, but still I make time to work on my portfolio. You must allow psychological space to work on your portfolio, every day. You must find qualified people to help you, and associate with those who have the same goals as you, so that the support you receive doesn't stop. You will be amazed at how your capacity to achieve more increases when you do these things.

Get your psychological house in order from the outset and the problems which arise along the way will be easily dealt with and overcome. Recognise what your own particular issues might be and develop strategies for dealing with them before you start. And never stop working toward your financial future – the road is long and tough, but remaining positive and committed, and dealing with your fears, is the only way you will ever start the journey.

Goals and roles

If you are buying with a spouse, partner or another person, don't start until you have a lengthy discussion about goals and roles. Decide together what you want to achieve and ensure your plans match. This includes a discussion about exit strategies which is most important when your investing partner is not your life partner and so may have a different investing time horizon. It's crucial that everyone starts on the same page with a crystal clear picture of the shared goal.

Write your strategy and goals down and formulate a contract upon which you all agree. Make sure all contingencies have been considered and noted, and all parties are given a copy of this 'contract'.

And finally, agree on the roles you will all take. Many an investing strategy has stalled when the parties step on each other's toes, or don't play their role to the satisfaction of the other(s). Having a written plan of action which identifies roles and tasks can be a valuable document if trouble arises.

KEY POINTS

~ Procrastination results in time wasted and opportunity lost.

~ Most fears, when examined, are extremely unlikely to eventuate.

~ Lack of motivation is a big enemy which must be addressed.

~ Make property education and exposure a part of every day.

~ Set goals and roles, in writing, at the outset.

14

THE LATEST
CLEVER SCHEMES
AND SCAMS

In my writing and on my television shows, I often warn of the various schemes and scams which are on offer for property investors. Just as I think I've come to the last of them, new ones emerge and property investors must remain ever vigilant to ensure that they are not trapped.

A few months ago, Arthur emailed me to tell of his discontent with a service for which he had paid $15,000. He was somewhat sheepish in admitting that, while he sees himself as astute and careful, he had been swayed by the promises of this company, the head of which had written a book and so had acquired some credibility in the property industry.

In a nutshell, Arthur had been promised one-to-one mentoring which would significantly accelerate his investing success and, as these companies often promise, launch him into millionaire status in a short timeframe. Through a succession of workshops and telephone meetings, Arthur would be provided with the secrets he needed to realise his dreams of wealth.

Of course, as you have probably guessed, Arthur quickly discovered that there are no secrets, and after attending a number of unenlightening seminars and receiving a few rushed 15 minute mentoring calls, Arthur's disillusionment was complete. He had discovered that his mentor was probably only a few steps ahead of him and had no secrets to tell at all, apart from the stunning revelation that he needed to find property with growth of more than 12% per annum!

Well, of course, that would be lovely wouldn't it? If only we could all just pluck areas which will return 12% per annum, every year, then we'd all be rich in a short period of time. But the truth was that this company, like so many others, was making millions themselves from the mentor fees of investors just like Arthur, and their own property portfolio is likely the result of this windfall, rather than their own investing prowess.

You most likely read this and think that you would be less gullible than Arthur, but I know for a fact that Arthur is intelligent and enquiring. He's just really busy, and the chance to have someone, whose marketing is brilliant, do the hard work for him made him vulnerable to their promises and easily led in that instance. Luckily for Arthur, he was able to have his fees refunded, but not without a considerable battle in which all manner of legal action was threatened. In the end, it was quietly settled, meaning that this company lives to rip off more people like Arthur.

> If only we could all just pluck areas which will return 12% per annum, every year, then we'd all be rich in a short period of time.

I am not for a moment suggesting that you should not seek a mentor, or even pay for good quality education. I am suggesting, however, that as there are no secrets to be revealed, such mentoring and education should represent value for money and be provided by people who truly have the runs on the board. I know of several experts who have vast experience and skills in the area of property investing, who also provide value-for-money courses and assistance, and who are genuinely in the business of helping others, rather than being in the business of amassing their own fortunes.

So, here now, is the latest list of things to watch out for. Some are schemes, and others are scams. It will be up to you to ascertain if any of them are right for you.

Hybrid Discretionary trusts

There have been entire companies set up solely for the purpose of creating Hybrid Discretionary trusts as vehicles for the purchase of property by individuals. It can be a minefield trying to read not only the definitions of what such a trust actually is, but how the tax office views one, and what real benefit they produce. I read everything I can and I still come away with my head in a spin regarding what this is really all about.

So, to put it simply, and to give you just enough information to explain why I am against the use of them, here is a quick definition.

A Hybrid Discretionary trust is a trust structure which combines the features of two different kinds of trusts: a discretionary (family) trust and a unit trust (see diagram overleaf). In earlier times, and to protect assets, people would often set up family trusts. Using this trust they would borrow to buy property, and, as they did not own the property, it was protected from creditors. Further, being a discretionary trust, decisions could be made as to how to distribute income every year, and children could be made beneficiaries to allow income to be distributed to those who had the lowest income rates.

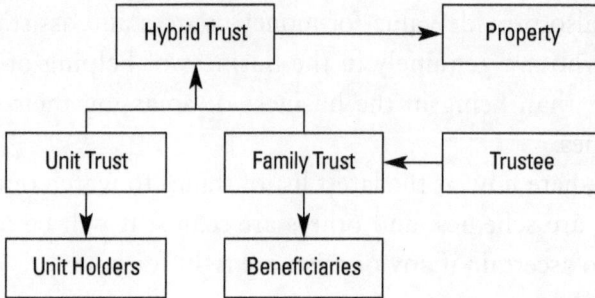

The problem with such trusts was that a family trust could not claim any negative gearing benefits, since it is not a tax paying entity. You can't claim tax benefits when you don't pay tax in the first place.

And so the Hybrid Discretionary trust was formed. In this arrangement, a family trust is established alongside a unit trust. The investor borrows money, and buys units in that unit trust, and the money raised via the sale of these units is then used to buy property. An instant space is created between the investor and the entity which owns the assets (the trust) and, as such, there is the capacity to protect assets.

…a family trust could not claim any negative gearing benefits.

Note that the investor has *not* purchased the property – rather they have purchased units in the entity (the trust) which owns the property. This is why, if sued, the property cannot be seized to satisfy creditors – the investor has no ownership of the property. Further, it is said that the loan which the investor obtains to buy the units is tax deductible, as it has bought units as an 'investment', just as one would if they bought units in a property trust or managed fund. It's a sneaky way to allow negative gearing benefits on funds borrowed, since those funds are 'invested' in a trust.

When you read about such trusts, the benefits will be listed as being:

~ Your assets will be protected from events like bankruptcy, insolvency and other legal challenges for your assets.
~ It is a relatively low cost and simple structure to use.
~ It allows you to distribute income to family members who are on low tax rates.
~ There is an absence of any formal legislative framework, such as the Corporations Law, to control the activities of the trustee.
~ It allows you to 'stream' income: you can distribute one type of income to one person and another type of income to another person.
~ Unit holders can claim a deduction for the interest incurred on the cost of their units if they borrowed to buy them.

It all sounds great and also pretty straightforward – once you buy the units, you should be able to simply claim the interest on any loan you acquire, since you are making an investment, right?

Well the tax office doesn't always see it like that, and recently there have been private rulings disallowing claims for all of the interest paid on any loan, on the basis that there are often several beneficiaries to such a trust, and the claimant doesn't have the right to all of the income or growth (and so should not have the right to claim all of the interest). While each individual ruling can and will be different, it's important for you to understand at this stage that such an arrangement is being closely looked at and, so far, the results have not been overly favourable to the investor.

The tax office's first concern in any scheme of arrangement will always be your dominant purpose. If your purpose for setting up any scheme, or entering into any arrangement, is to obtain a tax benefit, it's unlikely it will be allowed. A Hybrid Discretionary trust is expensive to set up and quite convoluted, and I cannot see how you would be able to prove that you were setting this up for the predominant purpose of anything other than a tax benefit.

In addition to this, following are some reasons why I don't like any arrangement which serves to separate a property investor from absolute ownership of a property asset:

~ As well as the interest expense, there are other claims which can really help with cash flow in those early years of an investment, when you need them most – such as depreciation. You will want the property in your own name, so you can maximise those deductions and use the extra tax you get back to cycle into debt repayment, thus gaining equity, which enables more property buying, faster.

~ ASIC and the Family Court can both unwind a trust structure to seize assets where they believe that you have set one up 'in contemplation of being sued'. Let's face it, if it's asset protection you are after, then you are contemplating being sued. If it's a tax benefit, then the tax office won't allow the claim.

~ At the commencement of a property portfolio, most properties will not make much money in the form of cash flow, so there is little to distribute anyway, and creating one may lose those depreciation benefits. Toward the end, however, when money *is* being made, you will want to benefit from that by having it distributed to you (isn't the ultimate income the reason why you buy property?). When you take a distribution, it is tacked on to the top of anything else you earn that year and taxed accordingly, and so you haven't really avoided paying tax, you've just deferred it.

~ For those who think they will include their children to minimise tax payable when the income is distributed, consider this: firstly, your children are likely to be working by the time you do this, and they will probably be paying tax at your rate anyway, and secondly, who wants all of their hard earned income going to the kids?

Further to this, I asked Julia Hartman, from Bantacs, who is perhaps the most knowledgeable person I have ever met when it comes to all kinds of property tax issues and tax office rulings, and she said this:

> 'In my opinion, hybrids don't provide anything they promise, particularly asset protection, just because you own the units instead of the property. If your creditors get hold of the units, then they can access the property anyway. If the hybrid promoter claims to have a clause to protect the unit holder from creditors, this very same clause will prevent the interest on the money borrowed for the units from being fully tax deductible, because there is another purpose achieved. Normally, the tax office position is that deductions

are allowed only up to the amount of the net rent – that is, there is no negative gearing allowed.'

You must be careful of those who are giving you advice about these arrangements, as I have seen some really bad advice imparted.

Marie, a close friend of mine, had a Hybrid Trust implemented for her and her husband by a very well known company who have been marketing these things for a few years now. When she showed it to me, I realised that this company had suggested that she buy her own family home within this trust and then have her highly paid husband buy the units in the trust which owned that home. She had been advised that the interest on the loan obtained to buy these units was fully tax deductible (as the loan bought investment units, rather than her own home), and that this smoke and mirrors approach would turn what would have been a non-tax deductible debt to buy her own home, into a tax-deductible one because it only bought units in the trust.

All taxpayers remain responsible for their own tax affairs.

I don't think the tax office has caught up with her yet, but this has as much chance of being approved as I have of seeing pigs flying past my window! Sadly, she took this advice at face value, since these people have published a book and even write columns in property magazines, and so they have the appearance of legitimacy. Further, when she is fined or forced to find the money to pay back taxes, those setting up this structure for her will have no penalty, as all taxpayers remain responsible for their own tax affairs, even when a professional assists them.

To be honest, I can't see any true benefits that can be achieved by making your life as complex as it would be if you set up such a trust. You will most certainly have increased accounting costs by having a trust in place, and any real asset protection benefits are questionable and largely untested. I have never met anyone yet who has been sued to any great degree, and I'd like to suggest that this is not as big a concern as the pundits of such structures make out.

Stick with buying as an individual, where you can legally reduce your tax, and work toward an uncomplicated and profitable future.

Self managed superannuation funds (SMSFs)

This is the new kid on the block, and it didn't take long for the hungry opportunists to jump on this band wagon and set up at property shows all over the country promoting the use of a self managed superannuation funds to buy property.

Why is this? My theory is that these people, who benefit from both the fees to set up the funds and the commission on the property they subsequently sell to that fund, saw very quickly that, while some people did not have the equity or borrowing capacity to buy a property in their own name, those same people may well have significant funds tied up in public superannuation funds, which could be accessed legally by setting up their own funds. This then increased the number of people to whom property could be sold, and provided a brand new market for their property products.

I am not against a self managed superannuation fund for the right person, as long as it has been set up under the right circumstances. However I believe that there are significant drawbacks, many of which are never outlined during the selling phase, that all investors must be aware of before they make the possibly incorrect decision to set up one. Here are just a few.

Borrowing

Changes to the Superannuation Industry Supervision (SIS) Act in September 2007 now mean SMSFs can borrow to purchase real estate, using a structure established for this purpose, as long as certain conditions are met. There are various loan products offered which enable these purchases to be made.

There are a number of issues with these loans:

~ It is not a straight loan to the superannuation fund – there must be a trustee who buys the property on behalf of the fund, who becomes the legal owner, while the superannuation fund becomes the beneficial owner – that is, the entity which benefits from the asset.

~ Loans to superannuation funds are known as non-recourse loans. This means that, if the loan is not repaid, the capacity of the lender to recover the outstanding money is limited to what they can recover by selling the property which those funds bought. They cannot touch any other fund assets. This seems good on the surface, but it means that the loan to valuation ratios are usually quite low, around 60%, to allow a suitable margin to pay costs and to account for any falls in the market value. This means that the super fund will need to have the remainder of the purchase price, plus costs available.

~ Each security property can only be used once – even if

it grows significantly in value, its equity cannot be leveraged into further property. This means that each time a super fund buys a property, it must have the cash available to cover 40% of the purchase price, plus costs. If you consider that most people have less than $100,000 in superannuation, this means that their super fund can probably buy only one property. I consider the major strength of a property investing strategy is the ability to compound growth through leverage, and one property does very little for your financial future.

There are some benefits too:

~ As a trust structure, assets within this fund can pass more easily to beneficiaries.

~ If you own your own business you can borrow to buy your business' real property (but not operating assets) using the super fund.

~ You will pay a maximum 10% capital gains tax upon eventual sale of a property, and if the property is sold during the pension phase there is no CGT.

~ You pay a maximum 15% income tax on rental income.

~ Other super fund assets are secure as the lender does not have recourse to the other assets.

~ Interest expenses may be claimed as tax deductions by the SMSF, which can potentially reduce your SMSF's tax liability.

To set up and run your own SMSF, it is required by law for the SMSF to be a complying fund. You will need to consult with a financial adviser to check on the eligibility of your fund under the SIS Act. Severe penalties apply for non compliance under this Act.

In addition, you have to have an articulated investment strategy in place. It must reflect the purpose and circumstances of the fund and take into account:

~ How to maximise its member returns, while taking into account the risk;
~ Diversification of the long-term investment strategy; and
~ The ability of the fund to pay benefits as members retire, as well as other expenses incurred by the fund.

If a fund becomes non-complying, its income tax rate will go up to 45%, and it will also incur 45% tax on all of its assets, at the start of each year that it is in breach. This will cause the fund to have a tax bill it probably can't pay, and this may cause the property to be sold.

Remember also that for many, property is a long-term hold, and eventual sale may not even feature, which will reduce some of the benefits that buying a property using a SMSF may bring in the short term.

You can't live in any property that your super fund buys and you can't rent one from your super fund, so the idea of buying a holiday home for your own use is out. You also cannot transfer personal assets into a superannuation fund, and so there is no opportunity for your super fund to take ownership of any residential property you already own.

On balance, I think there is little benefit to be gained from the average person setting up a self managed super-annuation fund for the principal objective of investing in property. The compliance procedures to ensure that your fund isn't in breach of legislation can be costly and cumbersome, and these added costs can reduce some of the other benefits significantly.

Wealth creation websites

Recently, I received an emailed from a concerned *Property Success* viewer who had seen my photo and biography featured on a website alongside a number of 'infamous' property 'experts' – you know, the kind who *A Current Affair* is always chasing down the street, and who answer each question with 'no comment', or hide in the ladies room to avoid difficult questions being posed by disgruntled followers.

This website listed five people amongst their 'expert dream team' and, lo and behold, there were my details, at number three! Upon further reading it was clear that I wasn't actually appearing anywhere with my alleged fellow dream team members, and I could tell that the information and photo had been ripped from another legitimate site elsewhere. But, the point was made and anyone who knew little about these things would easily have thought that I had gone over to the dark side!

Enlisting a friend who is great at chasing down detail, we explored further and discovered that there exists a form of 'pyramid marketing for wealth creation sites'. We pieced the detail together and, to the best of our ability, this is how we think these things go.

An internet marketing seminar is promoted at a property investor seminar – anyone with a passion for property and something to say can enlist to learn (you guessed it!) *the secrets* of making money via the internet. The fee to attend such a marketing seminar is a few thousand dollars and as the return is promised as being exponential many sign up.

At this seminar, attendees are provided with a skeleton website to which they can add their own personality and they are taught how to use it to make money.

The resulting website, owned by the usually unsuspecting property investor, will have some kind of flashy name which infers the capacity to create boundless wealth, such as www. pathwaystoriches.com.au. www.millionairesinaminute.com. au. The websites are all similar in a number of ways. They usually offer four or five 'free gifts' if you sign up (believe it or not, I was allegedly offering one of these free gifts!), and the page detailing the 'dream team' contains many of those suspect experts I alluded to before.

There are also features where the website owner's own personality and expertise (if any) can be displayed – blogs, articles etc., and there is always the chance to buy product of some description – books, tapes and other investor tools. While all of the websites are different, they all have a visual similarity which is obvious once you visit a few – a sensationalist overtone and a lot of flashy, wild claims, inferring the potential for untold riches.

Poke them a little and they will fall apart, as there is little use to any of the information, and the people at the top of this pyramid are shamefully taking advantage of those who might otherwise simply have had some good intentions and the desire to be in their own business. The website that I was first made aware of which had my details (which turned out to be one of many) was owned by a nice young man who seemed genuinely hurt that I was angry, as he believed I was fully aware and agreeable to what was going on. He further volunteered that the people who set up the site for him, those who were coincidentally part of that dream team, had promised him commissions which he was still waiting for. I have spent a lot of money having lawyers chasing down such people and ensuring references to me are removed from such sites, and I trust that those who know me will also know that I will never plunge into any such misadventure. Sadly, some of those people who have sites such as these have gone on to offering the very mentoring and seminars which Arthur found useless, and regardless of how verbal I am, not a lot seems to be changing.

The best way for us to ensure that these kinds of opportunists don't profit any longer from these tactics is to stay educated and refuse to pay these ridiculously large sums of money for information from people whose backgrounds are questionable. Just because an expert can vaguely refer to a successful background or experience doesn't make it real – and many have no hard evidence that the success they claim to have even exists.

Anyone can publish a book and get a great looking website these days, yet that is simply no measure of their true capacity to guide you well.

As I said, you will need to spend some money to gain a good education and to get the right support team around you. Before you do, research as much as you can, ask for evidence of the success of the person offering you the help, and get testimonials from others who can show that they have actually succeeded themselves as a result of following the advice. Anyone can publish a book and get a great looking website these days, yet that is simply no measure of their true capacity to guide you well.

Experts

On Monday evenings, I host a show called *Your Money Your Call*, on the Sky News Business Channel (602). With a panel of experts, who I have personally chosen, we invite callers to phone in with any question they may have about property investing, and then we do our best to provide comprehensive answers. My pool of panel members is very small, because I frequently find that those who call themselves experts rarely are.

I am continuously contacted by PR companies suggesting guests for my show. You would be amazed to find that these days everyone has a PR company! Real estate agents, property advisers, analysts and economists, they all want to be on TV, and enlist the services of such a company to splash their identity about the place.

I've never had a PR company and think that if someone is using one it's often for their own benefit, rather than the benefit of those they claim to want to assist. I can understand an actor or model needing a PR company, since fame is their goal. But property advisers and experts should have the goal of assisting others, not of being recognised at airports.

Remember that property expertise and real knowledge and skill cannot be inferred upon a person simply because they write a book, have a great website or appear on TV with the mantle of 'expert' strapped under their picture. True property experts are those who have reliable and important information to give away, and they give it away because they believe in that information, not because they make money from it. While the ability to make a living out of one's expertise is most certainly acceptable (I do it!), I find it unpalatable for experts to charge sums of money inconsistent with the service they provide, as many property investment organisations seem to do today.

As I've said, you will need to pay for quality advice and the right kind of assistance. Before you do so, assess what you are getting against what is being paid. $15,000 for a year of telephone support, or a weekend course simply doesn't seem commensurate with what is being delivered.

Regulation

This may shock you, but, at the time of writing there still exists no regulation in the property investment industry. Technically, this means that anyone, regardless of their experience and qualifications, can give you advice on how to spend a considerable amount of money to buy an investment property, even making commissions from the sale and charging you for their advice, and not a single piece of legislation exists to offer you the tiniest amount of protection if it all goes wrong.

...at the time of writing there still exists no regulation in the property investment industry.

The government should be thoroughly ashamed of itself. The time and effort I have placed into trying to bring about such regulation, with the help of my fellow board members of the Property Investment Professionals of Australia (PIPA), have led me to believe that the government, and ASIC to a lesser degree, is more concerned with containing costs than they are with your financial security.

I have had meetings with Treasury and individual Senators, provided comment to newspaper articles and I have developed comprehensive submissions which practically hand the legislation to the government on a silver platter, and for five years I have been completely stone-walled.

Do I sound mad to you? You bet I am! If you have $20,000 cash to invest, your financial planner will be regulated to the wall in regards to how they can advise you on its investment. But, mention you are looking to buy $500,000 worth of property and every shonky man and his dog will come out of the woodwork to help you part with it, and you will be left stranded when it falls in a heap.

Recently, new regulation around mortgage brokers was introduced, and in response to a query by a journalist I know, made to the office of the Treasurer (addressed to Bill Shorten the then Assistant Treasurer and Minister for Financial Services and Superannuation) about the absence of Property Investment Adviser laws, a statement was issued by his office saying:

> "The Government is currently implementing numerous reforms, including the national regulation of consumer credit and the Competitive and Sustainable Banking System Package. These reforms will regulate property spruiking intermediaries who are involved in arranging credit for consumers."

I had to be held back from flying to Melbourne and shaking the Treasurer till he finally saw some sense! The ridiculous suggestion that the only problem in this industry comes from spruikers was only upstaged by the claim that regulating the people who write the finance for their dodgy deals was going to in any way make a difference.

The fact remains – as a property investor, you currently have no right to be protected in your dealings; if you receive bad advice which you act upon, you have no recourse. Further, your advisers are unlikely to even have Professional Indemnity Insurance, as the underwriters will not insure unregulated professionals.

PIPA (www.pipa.asn.au) is a not-for-profit association which is working hard to change this situation, and I promise you I do not intend to stop lobbying until we have a suitable outcome. In my opinion, the only suitable outcome is regulation and I will fight for that until I am very old if necessary. Meanwhile, PIPA has created standards and accreditation to ensure that someone is watching the shop. Our members are required to uphold a strict code of conduct and to also work toward becoming a Qualified Property Investment Adviser (QPIA®) by completing a course. This course was developed initially by Deakin Prime University and I have since undertaken significant upgrades to it.

You can help in two ways. Firstly you can email Bill Shorten (or whoever the Treasurer is when you are reading this), asking the simple question: "Why is there no regulation for the Property Investment Industry and when will it be introduced?" I figure that if everyone who reads this book does this, he'll get tens of thousands of emails and something will have to be done. Be sure that you tell him to contact PIPA, because we can help him to fast-track this issue. His email address is Bill.shorten@treasury.gov.au

Secondly, you can bring pressure to bear on the industry by refusing to deal with any property professional who is *not* a member of PIPA. Oh, when asked they are likely to give you a range of plausible reasons why they aren't, but the facts are membership to the association is not expensive, and we are not for profit.

Deal only with Qualified Property Investment Advisers.

Last of all, deal only with Qualified Property Investment Advisers (QPIA®), who have completed the PIPA course. No other course matches its high standards and at least by dealing with such people you can be sure of a high standard of service delivery and knowledge.

KEY POINTS

~ It is important to obtain quality guidance but be careful of the scammers.

~ Mentor support should not come at a ridiculous price.

~ There are no secrets to property investing so don't allow someone to fool you into paying thousands to get them.

~ Hybrid Discretionary trusts are being closely looked at by the Tax Office and many are not being allowed to claim as they would like.

~ Self managed super funds carry huge compliance requirements and are not really suitable for the average property investor.

~ Wealth creation websites of any description should be avoided or carefully scrutinised.

~ Writing a book does not make anyone an expert.

~ Guidance should be paid for, but at reasonable rates commensurate with what is being delivered, not what they promise that you can make by employing their strategies.

~ Until there is regulation you will need to be doubly cautious about any investment property professional.

15

START NOW AND DON'T STOP

I'm pretty sure that's it – for now at least! Once again I hope that, by telling you as much as I possibly can about how to invest well in property, those unqualified and dodgy experts who presently attempt to sell property secrets to you at exorbitant prices will have a reducing market of people to sell to.

Economic uncertainty is still a part of the general property investing landscape, and will be for most of your investing life, and that brings uncertainty about interest rates and housing affordability. Property investors must begin to fill their portfolios with the types of property which can in some way be recession-proof, which can remain relatively stable despite what the underlying economy may be doing.

Read the national press with only a passing interest and take care not to put too much stock into reporting by journalists. If it involves studies which have been done, get a hold of the study so you can see how in depth it was and if it is a true representation of the matters it was investigating. If it reports forecasts by economists, remember that usually 50% of economists are right and the other 50% are usually wrong. They, like so many data companies, are simply using historical data to forecast future events. Our economy has changed intrinsically forever, and much of the historical information available has become outdated and useless for forecasting trends of any kind. And besides, property rarely follows a trend, so spending hours trying to ascertain the next boom area by studying historical data is a waste of your valuable time.

Economic uncertainty is still a part of the general property investing landscape.

Take any marketing material about new property developments at face value and independently confirm all information which is contained therein. Don't allow newspaper reporting to paint a skewed picture about property market health, and understand that all markets will be different at any one time.

Learn about the economy. You, like me, may have hated economics lessons when you were at school, but there is no doubting the fact that, on a micro level, economic data can give us valuable information to assist with our property research. It can tell us what is growing and what is not, and even whether yields are likely to increase or fall.

And, as always, continue to be careful about who you get your information from. Many investment companies which may be selling a property to you will only provide information which is positive, and they will also only be presenting the best that they have available at the time. Such property may not suit your financial goals or risk profile, and there may well be property in other areas which is more suited to your own needs. Your search for property should be broad and include many sources, and care needs to be taken where sales commissions to property marketers aren't properly disclosed to you.

As I always say, the onus is on you, and you can go a long way toward protecting yourself. Educate yourself as much as you can before you start and continue to update your knowledge along the way. A sound understanding of how the overall economy ultimately impacts back in our property market is crucial, as is an ability to carry out thorough and comprehensive research.

APPENDIX
YOUR RISK PROFILE

The following questions will help you identify your risk profile as it applies to property investing. Select one answer in each section.

1. How would you describe yourself?
1. Retired and dependent on existing funds and/or pensions for income.
2. With a family to support. While you understand the need to invest, you cannot see how it will be possible, as your income is fully committed to the family budget.
3. Easily managing your current financial commitments. Your current income provides an acceptable lifestyle. You may be just starting out on your career or be well-established.
4. At the peak of your career and income, possibly with a dual income. You have no dependants and/or easily manage the expense needs of your dependants.

2. What is your understanding of investing in property?
1. Not very familiar with it.
2. You understand the need to invest, but little more.
3. You understand how different property types can produce differing income and growth.
4. You are an experienced investor with a current property portfolio.

3. **What are your financial goals?**
   1. Income from an investment is the most important outcome for you.
   2. Safety is the most important feature for you.
   3. You have a specific timeframe of, for example, five years and a set return you would like to achieve in that time.
   4. Growth is the most important outcome for you.

4. **If your investment property was to suddenly lose value by 20%, what would your reaction be?**
   1. You would sell up immediately and never invest in property again.
   2. You would keep what you had but not buy anymore.
   3. You would be concerned but would wait and see for a while before you invested again.
   4. You would not be concerned – you might even invest more in the same area while you can get a bargain!

5. **Which do you prefer?**
   1. Stable though relatively low returns.
   2. Consistent returns with minimal tax savings.
   3. Variable returns with good tax savings.
   4. Higher returns with maximum tax savings (but higher risk).

6. **When do you plan to retire?**
   1. Already retired.
   2. Within five years.
   3. In 5 to 15 years.
   4. In more than 15 years.

7. How often would you sell your property?

1. Never.
2. Within 10 years.
3. Every time there is a substantial gain.
4. Every year or two.

8. In relation to buying property sight-unseen, you feel:

1. You simply could not do it.
2. You may be able to do it if you had lots of pictures.
3. You would be happy to do so if you had someone you could trust to go and look at the property on your behalf.
4. You don't need to see it at all as long as the figures stack up.

Use the following formula to add up your score

- For every 1 answer, score one point.
- For every 2 answer, score two points.
- For every 3 answer, score three points.
- For every 4 answer, score four points.

Your Results

7–13 points: Conservative:

- You are a conservative investor who is risk adverse.
- You are prepared to sacrifice higher returns for peace of mind.
- You have a short-term investment period in which income and preserving your capital is of prime concern.
- You should only invest in low risk property which includes standard residential property in well populated city suburbs or large regional towns.
- You should ensure a low 'Loan to Valuation Ratio" (LVR), around 50-60 per cent.

14–20 points: Stable:
- You are a stable investor who is prepared to accept a small amount of risk.
- You are willing to take a small degree of short-term risk if it means the chance of long-term returns.
- Your investment term is three to five years.
- Security is very important to you though, and income is more important than growth.
- You should buy standard residential with a positive cashflow, and with sufficient research you may be able to buy in smaller towns with evidence of economic vibrancy such as mining towns.
- You can set your LVR between 60 – 80%.

21–27 points: Balanced:
- You are a balanced investor and have comfort with a moderate amount of risk.
- You have a relatively long period in which to invest.
- You are comfortable with short-term volatility for long-term growth and income.
- You would like some security but are prepared to take some risk.
- You usually invest in standard residential, and could invest short tern holiday let with standard management and some commercial premises such as offices with evidence of high demand and a positive cashflow.
- You can comfortably set your LVR at 80%.

28–32 points: Assertive:
- You are an assertive investor who is comfortable with higher levels of risk.
- You look for growth investments and are willing to include some speculative investments.
- You can cope with negative returns and increased volatility.
- Capital growth is your prime concern.
- You can invest in most types of property including inner city apartments or niche market properties such as serviced apartments and retirement villages (high income) as well as commercial properties including factories and warehouses.
- High income earners with a sufficient surplus may accept negative cash flow.
- You could stand up to a 90% LVR if necessary.

GLOSSARY OF TERMS

Australian Securities and Investments Commission (ASIC)
The Australian Securities and Investments Commission (ASIC) is an independent Commonwealth government body that regulates Australia's corporates, markets and financial services.

Blue Chip Properties These are thought to be Australia's most expensive properties in established up-market suburbs. The term 'blue chip' is also applied to some companies listed on the Australian Securities Exchange (ASX) where it refers to the largest, most stable companies; for example, BHP-Billiton, Woolworths and the four big banks. The blue chip in a casino has the highest value.

Borrower A party to a loan – the person borrowing the funds.

Capital Gains Tax (CGT) Capital gains tax (CGT) is a cost of investing. You pay CGT on the gain made upon the sale of an income-producing asset. The methods for calculating CGT may differ from time to time and depend upon when the asset was acquired.

Capital Works refers to any structural improvements or existing structure which form part of an investment property.

Cash Flow refers to the amount of money left over, or owing, once rent is collected, expenses are paid and tax claims are made. The amount will be either positive (if money is left) or negative (if money is owed).

Central Business District (CBD) This is the main commercial area of a city or large regional town. In recent years there has been an increase in residential property in CBD areas.

Company Title In rare cases, an original building is owned in a company title. Under this arrangement, you do not have ownership to a property title at all. Instead, you own shares in the company that owns the property. Usually, you still have some sort of levy to pay as there is still common property upkeep required.

Community Titles have only been around since 1989 and they are similar to a strata title. The difference is that a community title is commonly applied to a major land subdivision where common areas are provided for the enjoyment of the home owners in the subdivision.

Depreciation refers to the loss in value due to general wear and tear and the effects of time on the building, fixtures, fittings and furniture on an eligible, income-producing property. The property does not have to be new to make these claims, but the age of the property will affect both whether such claims are available to you, and what claims can be made. The website of the Australian Tax Office (www.ato.gov.au) includes a "Guide to Depreciation" which can be downloaded.

Developer The person providing the funds (personal or borrowed) and taking the risk for building a property for sale.

Equity The difference between what you owe and what you own of a property.

Extrinsic Growth Drivers are economic influences which contribute to the growth of an area but which originate outside of that area. They come from activity, planning and events which occur temporarily and bring short-term, unsustainable growth.

Fittings and Fixtures Items such as baths, stoves, lights and other fittings, kitchen, linen or storage cupboards and wardrobes. Fittings are not normally included in a contract if they can be removed without causing damage.

Forecast Assumptions made (often on paper by developers) about the future growth and income-earning potential of an investment, based on historical performance and projected future events.

Freehold Title An example of clear title. This means that once you buy the property you can be sure that no-one can come along and claim that the title is not yours (also see *Torrens Title, Green Title*).

Gearing means 'to borrow'. It is often used together with the qualifiers: 'negative' or 'positive' (please see *negative gearing* and *positive gearing*).

Global Financial Crisis (GFC) is the term used to describe the economic crisis which affected the entire world in 2008.

Green Title (in WA) This means that once you buy the property you can be sure that no-one can come along and claim that the title is not yours (also see *Torrens Title, Freehold Title*).

Gross Domestic Product (GDP) A term which describes the market value of all final goods and services produced within a country in a given period. It is often considered an indicator of a country's standard of living.

Gross Regional Product (GRP) measures the growth, or otherwise, of an entire region. A strong, growing GRP may be a precursor to other economic factors which ultimately drive property growth – more jobs, a growing population and increasing median household income.

Gross State Product (GSP) measures the growth, or otherwise, of an entire state.

Housing Starts This term refers to the number of new private dwellings where construction has commenced in a given period. It is most often measured quarterly.

Hybrid Discretionary Trusts This is a trust structure which combines the features of two different kinds of trusts: a discretionary (family) trust and a unit trust.

Interest The sum charged by the lender, calculated on the outstanding balance of borrowings, in deference to having supplied you with funds.

Intrinsic Growth Drivers are those factors which affect growth but which come from within an area and deliver sustainable growth. They are economic influences which are created by a complete set of circumstances, rather than single, individual events. They are influences which can be repeated and sustained over time and which are a sign of underlying economic growth.

Lease A document granting possession of a property for a given period without conferring ownership. The lease document specifies the terms and conditions of occupancy by the tenant.

Leverage The use of borrowed capital for investing.

Loan to Valuation Ratio (LVR) This is ratio which measures the percentage that a lender will lend a borrower in relation to what percentage of the loan the borrower will fund. For example, if the LVR on an investment property is 80% and the property is valued at $400,000, the lender will advance $320,000 and the borrower must fund $80,000 of the investment.

Macro Economy This is the economic 'big picture' based on national or state economic data.

Micro Economy This is the economic detail of the area where you are researching to buy; population growth; business; demographics; infrastructure plans of the area.

Mortgage The legal agreement on the terms and conditions of a loan for the purpose of buying real estate, whereby the person offering the mortgage takes security over the property.

Negative Gearing is not a 'strategy', it is a tax term to explain that expenses associated with borrowing to invest in an asset are greater than the income the investment asset generates.

Niche Market Property refers to any property which is purpose-built for a specific market, such as those built for tourists, seniors or students.

Occupancy The period that a tenant occupies a property.

Old System Title A very small minority of properties still come under the 'old system' title. These titles are hard to trace back and do not have a clear pathway of ownership through the years. As such, these titles are not guaranteed by the government. In rare cases, true original ownership could be challenged on such a property, and so in the event that you choose a property with such a title, be sure to get good legal advice.

On-Paper Deductions Tax claimable items which do not have a relative cash outlay.

Opportunity Cost This is the cost of a lost opportunity. For example, if an investor buys in one market it is at the lost opportunity of buying in another area that may have a different outcome. The cost is either justified, or not.

Positive Gearing is not a 'strategy', it is a tax term to explain that income generated by an investment asset is greater than the expenses incurred when borrowing to invest.

Positive Cash Flow is when you are left with money after you make all of your claims. This can happen if you negatively gear (and subsequently get a tax break big enough to make up the loss) or where you positively gear (where you are left with money after you have paid the tax on any income you have made).

Rent Guarantee A promise to pay a pre-agreed rent for a pre-agreed term.

Risk Profile An outline of the level of risk with which investors are comfortable. It is obtained according to their responses to questions on how they feel about investing and their personal investing choices.

Security Property offered to the mortgagee in return for a loan.

Self Managed Superannuation Funds (SMSFs) A self managed super fund (SMSF) is a trust established for one to four people where cash and investments are held for the principal purpose of funding the members' retirement. The costs of setting up a fund can be prohibitive and the compliance onerous.

Settlement Completion of sale (or advancing of a loan) when the balance of a contract price is paid to the vendor and the buyer is legally entitled to take possession of the property.

Shares Units of ownership in a publicly-listed company which can be traded on the stock exchange.

Strata Title Where a previously single block has been developed to house more than one residence, such as a block of flats or villas, seniors' accommodation complexes, or a hotel or serviced apartments, a strata title will be registered. By law, an owner's corporation, or body corporate, must be formed and every single owner given the right to membership of that entity.

Tax An amount of money paid to the government as a percentage of each dollar earned.

Tenant Either the person signing a lease to occupy premises or the description of a party to a property title.

Title (of property) The legal document recording a person's right to ownership of a property. There are various forms of title, with particular characteristics (also see *Freehold, Torrens Title, Green Title, Strata, Company, Community* and *Old System Title*).

Torrens Title This means that once you buy the property you can be sure that no-one can come along and claim that the title is not yours (also see *Freehold Title, Green Title*).

Vacancy Rate Refers to the percentage of the year which a property remains vacant. This is usually ascertained by determining the number of weeks the property is vacant as a percentage of the number of weeks in the year (52).

Vendor The person(s) or entity selling a property.

FURTHER READING
ALSO BY MARGARET LOMAS

How to Make Your Money Last as Long as You Do

This is the first book I ever wrote about positive cash flow property and it explains, in basic terms, what the concept is all about. In addition, it covers personal financial management, managing debt, rapid mortgage reduction, basic tax information and information about buying and selling real estate. It also looks in-depth at banks and borrowing.

You should read this book if you have a personal home loan debt that you would like to manage better, or if you are new to the world of property investing.

How to Make Your Money Last as Long as You Do is also available in a New Zealand edition that outlines New Zealand tax benefits.

How to Create an Income for Life

This book is the A to Z guide to investing in positive cash flow property and is without a doubt my most popular book. It covers in great depth the concepts of positive cash flow property, taxation information for investors, property management, loan structuring and property types and their risk ratings. It explores serviced apartments and other such unusual property types and looks at wealth protection.

You should read this book if you already have your personal debt under control and want to start, continue or change the way you put together a property portfolio.

How to Maximise Your Property Portfolio

Some people want to know more than their accountants and if this is you, this book is a must. It does not, however, replace the two previous books and depends upon you having already read at least one of them.

It covers the debate about cash flow and capital growth and puts the two into context. It provides advanced information about assessing cash flows and details body corporate information.

It also takes a look at niche market property and its place in a portfolio. The book then goes on to examine portfolio management and outlines exit strategies.

The tax information contained in *How to Maximise Your Property Portfolio* is more advanced and covers the methods of depreciation and low value pooling. It looks at structures such as companies and trusts, and explores which names property should be held in and why. Lastly, it looks at property management with a detailed section on recruiting a property manager.

You should read this book after you read one of the other two and when you have started to put together your property portfolio.

A Pocket Guide to Investing in Positive Cash Flow Property

This book relies on the fact that you have already gained the knowledge from reading the other books and it gives you a step-by-step guide to the actual buying process. Each chapter is a new step and once you have read the entire book you will own a property.

I use this book myself every time I make a new purchase, just to make sure that I do not miss any steps. It contains formulas, calculators, things to photocopy for your bank and lawyer, and a checklist at the end of each step to make sure you have completed the step fully.

The Truth about Positive Cash Flow Property

Once you have begun your journey and have either commenced buying property or are ready to go, this book is for you. This book relies on you having read one of the other books in the 'How To' series and completely understanding the concepts of positive cash flow investing, and it does not contain much of the detailed knowledge which is crucial if you are to be successful as an investor.

The aim of this book is to help to protect you against the many scams and dubious schemes which are so prolific today. In addition to uncovering the truth behind many of these, this book outlines the type of portfolio you do need in order to become financially secure, including examples of portfolios which everyday people can build safely and without too much risk. The book looks in depth at many of those complicated structures which are often suggested today, and details lending structures and some tax information. A book for those who are already on their way.

The 20 Must Ask Questions® for Every Property Investor

At a time when there is more information around for property buyers than ever before, investors are understandably confused about the best way to acquire property investments and build a portfolio which can satisfy future financial needs. This book aims to make all investors so savvy that opportunistic property spruikers have no market! It is about the research phase of the property investment process, and aims to equip all investors with so much knowledge that they will be able to lessen the risk of making poor choices and feel comfortable about buying in any market. Unlike my other books, it does not cover financing or conveyancing, tax issues or any other peripheral steps. It is purely my infamous 20 research questions, in depth, so that you can be sure that your property research is comprehensive and all-encompassing.

ABOUT DESTINY® FREE STUFF

1. Destiny® VIP

Becoming a Destiny® VIP is free, and doing so means you'll receive:

~ A free copy of the e-Report "7 Steps to Financial Independence through Property Investing"

~ Access to the Members Area of the Destiny® website.

~ A free monthly newsletter written by Margaret Lomas containing an abundance of up-to-date property news.

~ Ability to purchase tickets to Margaret Lomas seminars at a discount on the general admission prices.

~ Access to other discounts and special offers from time to time.

Just go to www.destiny.com.au and go to the VIP page.

2. Free Download

To access a simple calculator to help you calculate property cash flows before you buy, go to www.destiny.com.au and go to 'Download Finsoft'. You will need your book barcode to access this download.

3. *Your Money Your Call*

To view past episodes of Margaret's weekly live TV Show, *Your Money Your Call* (on Sky News Business every Monday night) visit www.destiny.com.au and go to the 'media' page.

4. Media Articles

Margaret writes and contributes to many media articles. To read past articles visit www.destiny.com.au and go to the 'media' page.

▷ Destiny®

Destiny Financial Solutions can assist you with a range of investment needs, as follows:

1. Advice and Support

Make the right decisions, and reach your goals sooner. Advice and support from qualified experts equates to less mistakes and a faster, less turbulent path to success. All Destiny® advisers are Qualified Property Investment Advisers (QPIA®) with years of experience in the property investment industry. Many have substantial property portfolios themselves, so you can be sure you will receive the right advice from people who are both qualified and educated.

2. Property Finance

The correct finance structure is vital. Property investors frequently underestimate the importance of finance selection and structuring when purchasing a property, regularly missing tax minimisation and debt reduction opportunities. Destiny® is a specialist in investment finance, and our free, comprehensive finance acquisition and structuring service ensures each property you buy is financed correctly the first time.

3. Structured Education

Knowledge is key to success. Developed by industry expert and Destiny® founder, Margaret Lomas, and delivered by our experienced network of branch managers, the Destiny® Essential Property Education course offers a fast-track to property investment skills acquisition through face-to-face training and a comprehensive course guide, ensuring that you emerge with the knowledge to invest, safely and successfully.

4. Investment Teams

Two heads are better than one. Destiny® Property Action Teams offer you access to like-minded and motivated property investors, sharing their knowledge and experience while you continually build your property portfolio. Goal-setting, monthly team sessions, and plenty of guided peer support enhances your property investment skills and ensures you stay focused and motivated.

Do you want to know more? Visit www.destiny.com.au to find the details of your nearest Destiny® branch or make an appointment.

5. Margaret Lomas Seminars

Each year Destiny® hosts seminars presented by Margaret Lomas, founder of Destiny, in those cities which have a Destiny® branch.

These seminars, which are usually two hours in duration, are full of relevant and up-to-date information to assist you with your property investing, and all attendees are given ample opportunity to present their questions to Margaret and clarify any points from her books which may be unclear.

Dates of upcoming seminars can be found by visiting www.destiny.com.au and visiting the Events page.

6. Destiny Online Store

Margaret has developed a range of products such as podcasts, e-books, conference DVDs and subscriptions to her show *Property Success with Margaret Lomas*. To view any of these products, visit www.destiny.com.au and go to the online store.

7. DestinyLive

DestinyLive.com.au is a comprehensive online resource and powerful tool set for anyone investing in property. Created by property investors for property investors means it has everything you need to become a successful property investor.

~ *Track the performance of your investment properties.*
  DestinyLive enables you to manage and track your

investment properties online, anywhere, anytime. Whether you have one property, a large portfolio or preparing for your first purchase, you have real time access to the information and complex calculations that matter.

~ *Learn from the experts.* With DestinyLive's media portal you can leverage the vast knowledge and years of experience of industry veterans such as Margaret Lomas. With hundreds of hours of searchable video and audio content, you can find the answers or learn anywhere, anytime, and at your own pace.

To learn more about this invaluable online resource visit www.destinylive.com.au and review the Tour pages.

If you would like to tell us how you felt about this book, or make a suggestion for future books, please contact: margaret.lomas@destiny.com.au

Destiny® Financial Solutions Pty Ltd
PO Box 5400
Chittaway Bay NSW 2261
Ph: 1800 648 640
www.destiny.com.au

INDEX